Office *of the* Comptroller *of the* Currency

Annual Report | Fiscal Year 2011

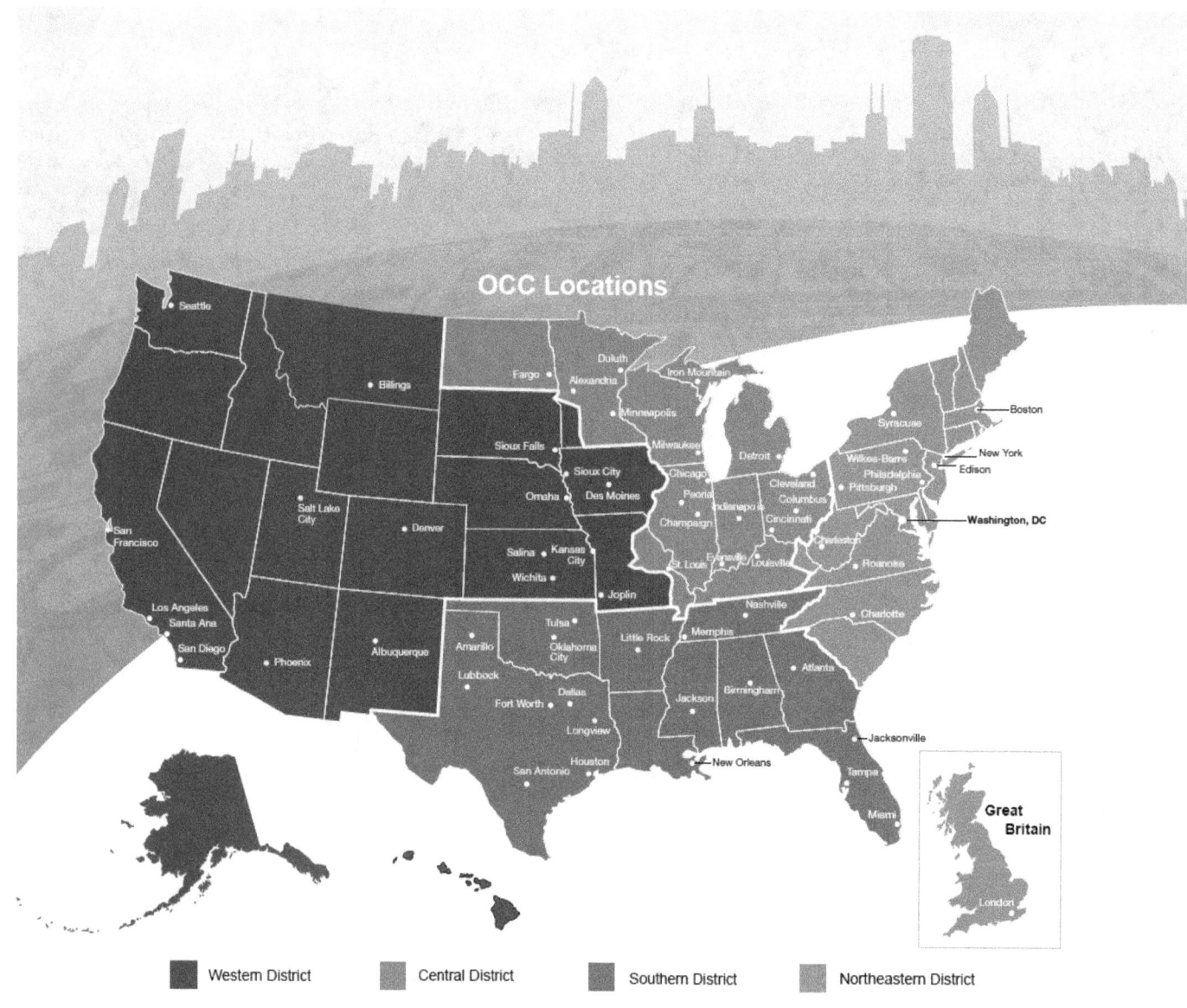

OCC Locations

Seattle · Billings · Fargo · Duluth · Alexandria · Iron Mountain · Boston · Syracuse · New York · Edison · Minneapolis · Sioux Falls · Milwaukee · Detroit · Wilkes-Barre · Philadelphia · Pittsburgh · Chicago · Cleveland · Columbus · Cincinnati · Washington, DC · Salt Lake City · Denver · Sioux City · Des Moines · Omaha · Peoria · Indianapolis · Charleston · San Francisco · Salina · Kansas City · St. Louis · Evansville · Louisville · Roanoke · Wichita · Joplin · Nashville · Charlotte · Los Angeles · Santa Ana · Tulsa · Little Rock · Memphis · San Diego · Oklahoma City · Albuquerque · Amarillo · Phoenix · Lubbock · Dallas · Jackson · Birmingham · Atlanta · Fort Worth · Longview · Jacksonville · San Antonio · Houston · New Orleans · Tampa · Miami

Great Britain — London

Western District · Central District · Southern District · Northeastern District

National Banking System at-a-Glance	
All OCC-supervised institutions	2,036
Large banks	45
Midsize banks	51
Community banks	1,303
Federal savings associations	637
All OCC-supervised institutions, total assets	$9.6 trillion
All OCC-supervised institutions, share of total U.S. commercial banking assets	76 percent

OCC at-a-Glance	
Employees (full-time equivalents)	3,717
Office locations*	66
Budget authority	$876.5 million
Revenue derived from assessments	97 percent
Consumer complaints opened	87,000
Consumer complaints closed	92,000

*The OCC maintains multiple locations in some large cities. In addition, the OCC has a continuous on-site presence at large banks under its supervision.

Agency Profile and History

The Office of the Comptroller of the Currency's (OCC) mission is to charter, regulate, and supervise all national banks and federal savings associations (collectively, banks) and to supervise the federal branches and agencies of foreign banks. In supervising banks, the OCC's goal is to ensure that they operate in a safe and sound manner and in compliance with laws requiring fair treatment of their customers and fair access to credit and financial products. The OCC is an independent bureau of the U.S. Department of the Treasury.

The President nominates the Comptroller of the Currency subject to confirmation by the U.S. Senate. The Comptroller also serves as a director of the Federal Deposit Insurance Corporation (FDIC) and NeighborWorks America.

When John Dugan, the 29th Comptroller of the Currency, completed his five-year term in August 2010, John Walsh became Acting Comptroller of the Currency.

Headquartered in Washington, D.C., the OCC has four district offices plus an office in London, which supervises the international activities of national banks. The OCC's nationwide staff of examiners conducts on-site reviews of banks and provides sustained supervision of these institutions' operations. Examiners analyze loan and investment portfolios, funds management, capital, earnings, liquidity, sensitivity to market risk for all banks, and compliance with consumer banking laws governing banks with less than $10 billion in assets. The OCC examiners review internal controls, perform internal and external audits, and ensure compliance with law. They also evaluate management's ability to identify and control risk.

In supervising banks, the OCC has the power to

- examine the banks;
- approve or deny applications for new charters, branches, capital, or other changes in corporate or banking structure;
- take supervisory actions against banks that do not comply with laws and regulations or that otherwise engage in unsound practices;
- remove officers and directors, negotiate agreements to change banking practices, and issue cease-and-desist orders as well as civil money penalties; and

Abraham Lincoln

Salmon P. Chase

Hugh McCulloch

- issue rules and regulations, legal interpretations, and corporate decisions governing investments, lending, and other practices.

The OCC and the national banking system were created by the National Currency Act, which President Abraham Lincoln signed into law on February 25, 1863. In June 1864, the law was substantially revised and expanded and given a new name: the National Bank Act. It remains the basic statute under which the OCC and the national banking system operate today.

The first Comptroller of the Currency was Hugh McCulloch, formerly the president of the state-chartered Bank of Indiana. McCulloch went to Washington to argue against passage of the National Currency Act but soon came to appreciate its merits. Salmon P. Chase, Lincoln's Secretary of the Treasury, asked him to lead the new system, and McCulloch agreed.

Under McCulloch, his successors, and a professional staff of national bank examiners, the new system made an important contribution to the robust growth of the U.S. economy. National banks under OCC supervision issued a uniform national currency, which replaced the previous varied and unreliable money supply, and provided financial services all across the country.

The National Bank Act endows the OCC with considerable operational independence. The OCC does not receive appropriations from Congress. Instead, the OCC's operations are funded primarily through assessments on national banks. National banks pay additional fees for the OCC to process charter, merger, and other corporate applications.

On July 21, 2011, under provisions of the Dodd–Frank Wall Street Reform and Consumer Protection Act of 2010,[1] the Office of Thrift Supervision (OTS) became part of the OCC. As a result, the OCC is responsible for the supervision of federal savings associations, under the Home Owners' Loan Act.

---

[1] Hereafter referred to as Dodd–Frank in this report.

Contents

Comptroller's Viewpoint

When I signed the "Comptroller's Viewpoint" last year as Acting Comptroller of the Currency, it was with no expectation that I would do so again in 2011. Implementation of Dodd–Frank was just getting under way and looked to be the dominant theme for the next year and beyond. And indeed it has been dominant, but other events—other echoes of the financial crisis—have intervened to make this an even busier year than anyone could have imagined.

Almost every area of financial regulation was affected by events of the year, often in very significant ways. As expected, Dodd–Frank implementation was the major preoccupation of the OCC, especially the provisions that became effective in July 2011. New Basel initiatives in the areas of capital and liquidity—especially heightened standards for systemically important banks—expanded, and in some ways complicated, the Dodd–Frank reform agenda. Then the foreclosure mess came to light, resulting in a series of major enforcement actions to address failures in mortgage servicing and foreclosure processing. As we work to put regulation after regulation in place to create a future free of crisis, it is impossible to avoid recalling similar efforts after the savings and loans crisis 20 years ago. The lesson of economic

history seems to be that we are doomed to repeat it. But whatever questions there may be about the likely impact of the reform program, the implementation task is clearly far from over.

The sweeping Dodd–Frank Act will bring changes in the operations of large banks and the way the agencies monitor and manage systemic risk. In addition, the law mandated new regulations aimed at curbing abuses in mortgage lending and securitization that helped bring on the financial crisis. In all, Dodd–Frank set in motion nearly 100 projects at the OCC, including a yearlong effort to remake the agency by absorbing most of the staff and responsibilities of the OTS. That single requirement not only reshaped the agency but also greatly expanded our supervisory and regulatory presence in the area of mortgage lending.

After a year spent working on interagency rulemakings to implement Dodd–Frank, most of that work remains unfinished and a number of the ambitious deadlines in the law have been missed. Not so the transfer of staff and responsibilities from the OTS into the OCC. I'm pleased to report that we worked our way through the logistical and policy challenges involved in the integration, and 670 OTS employees reported to

work at OCC offices throughout the country on Monday, July 18, 2011, ahead of the official July 21 transfer date.

I have spent considerable time thanking our combined staffs for accomplishing all this so smoothly, but let the record show that the only simplification of the U.S. regulatory framework mandated by Dodd–Frank was achieved without fanfare—essentially without notice by the outside world. Our goal was to make the transition as smooth as possible, both for the federally chartered thrifts that were subject to OTS oversight and for the staff of the OTS that joined the OCC, and that was accomplished. We need every bit of the talent and experience of former OTS staff to help fulfill our combined supervisory mission, and the men and women joining us from the OTS have been fully integrated into policy and field units where their talents can best be utilized.

We also recognized at the outset how important it would be to pursue outreach to the thrift industry, and we established a robust communication program to ensure that thrift executives knew what to expect from the combined agency. We held 17 outreach meetings around the country, attended by more than 1,000 thrift executives. That program was supplemented by letters to thrift chief executive officers, outreach at the district level, Web postings, and other actions that made information available to the industry. Feedback we have received indicates that these efforts were successful in smoothing the transition for the thrift industry.

Another of our challenges was to move the entire body of OTS regulations into the OCC regulatory framework. Most of this was good housekeeping, conforming and streamlining the rule books, but our new, uniform preemption rule for banks and thrifts proved highly controversial. The former OTS preemption standard was repealed in favor of the OCC standard, as directed by Dodd–Frank. The key issue was whether Dodd–Frank had upended the basic conflict-preemption standard for national banks embodied in the *Barnett* Supreme Court decision or left it intact. We believe the standard was preserved and asserted our conclusion in a revised preemption regulation that attracted some criticism. I am happy to report that three federal court cases so far have reached the same conclusion about the impact of Dodd–Frank on the *Barnett* preemption standard. Preemption for national banks as we know it is preserved.

We also worked closely with the Consumer Financial Protection Bureau (CFPB), the new agency created by Dodd–Frank, to ensure that it had the information and support it needed to start up on July 21, 2011. Because the CFPB has such important responsibilities for rulemaking across the financial system and compliance supervision

for large banks and previously unregulated nonbanks, it is vital that we and the other bank regulatory agencies develop an effective working relationship with them. A key concern we expressed during the legislative process was to ensure an appropriate balance between safety and soundness and consumer protection, and that will require serious attention to the interagency consultation obligations of the CFPB that are built into Dodd–Frank. We have signed a number of memoranda of understanding regarding information sharing and collaboration, and I am hopeful these will prove effective in guiding our future working relationship.

At the same time, the OCC has participated actively in the Financial Stability Oversight Council, or FSOC, the intergovernmental body created by Dodd–Frank to identify risks to the financial system, extend supervision to systemically significant nonbanks, and respond to emerging threats to financial stability. I truly believe that this will be one of the most significant reforms mandated by Dodd–Frank. By bringing together agencies with responsibilities for every sector of the financial services industry, FSOC will examine risks across the entire financial system and help to avert future financial crises.

Among the other Dodd–Frank issues pending as we moved into the new fiscal year that began on October 1, 2011, were two exceptionally complicated rule-makings—risk retention and the "Volcker rule." These two rules

will have a dramatic impact on the way financial institutions serve consumers and businesses.

Clearly, one of the root causes of the financial crisis was poor credit underwriting, particularly in the area of subprime mortgages, and securitization fueled that surge in bad lending by transferring risk from the originator of the loan to other investors. Congress responded by requiring that sponsors of asset-backed securitizations retain at least 5 percent of the credit risk. An exception was made for loans that are underwritten to very high standards, such as qualified residential mortgages (QRM). While the standards proposed for the QRM have proven highly controversial, it is important to remember that the QRM was intended to be an exemption from risk retention, and not a comprehensive new mortgage underwriting standard.

In fact, Dodd–Frank was emphatic in calling for most lending to be subject to risk retention, and, at the end of the day, as the securitization market regains its footing, it is likely that will be the case. While the proposed rule was drafted to provide flexibility, all of the risk retention options in the proposal were designed to create financial disincentives against packaging loans that are poorly underwritten. The draft rule has proven highly controversial, and there is much work remaining before it can be put in final form.

The "Volcker rule" presents similar challenges. The premise behind this Dodd–Frank provision was simple: Congress believed that banks and bank holding companies were taking excessive risks by engaging in proprietary trading and investing in hedge funds and private equity funds, and these activities should be prohibited. The draft proposal was anything but simple: It is very hard to distinguish some prohibited activities from permitted market making and permissible investments. So the rule runs to almost 300 pages and includes nearly 400 questions on issues still to be resolved. All of us would like a simpler rulemaking, but the fact is that these distinctions are not easily drawn and going too far would cause unintended damage to the system.

In terms of impact, it would be impossible to ignore the changes that are under way affecting bank capital. We have not yet finished implementing Basel II, but the financial crisis highlighted weaknesses in capital policy that resulted in development of increased capital for market risk—so called Basel II.5—and overall increases in minimum capital requirements under Basel III. In addition to raising the amount of capital that banks must hold, setting an international leverage limit, and directing new liquidity standards, the Basel III standards also call for improvements in the quality of capital by requiring that Tier 1 capital consist almost exclusively of common equity. In September 2011, the Basel Committee on Banking Supervision agreed to add a surcharge of up to 2.5 percent for large and systemically important banks. These Basel III initiatives will apply to U.S. banks when U.S.

regulators promulgate revisions to U.S. capital regulations that embody the new standards.

Dodd–Frank also addressed capital and covered some of the same ground as the Basel Committee. The law requires more stringent prudential standards, including capital and liquidity requirements, for larger, more systemically important bank holding companies, and touches upon the quality of regulatory capital by limiting the use of certain hybrid instruments in capital calculations. Dodd–Frank also established specific requirements related to the leverage ratio, and it mandated studies on contingent capital.

It will be a challenge to implement all of these objectives in a sensible way, in part because the two frameworks are complicated, and in part because they do not always mesh well together. But we are working very hard on an interagency basis to make these new requirements work.

Finally, the OCC has devoted very significant resources to addressing the deficiencies in mortgage servicing and foreclosure processing that were revealed in late 2010—the first quarter of this fiscal year.

The volume of problem mortgages overwhelmed the capacities of the larger mortgage servicers, and shoddy practices like "robo-signing" resulted. Bank managers failed to pay enough attention to how simple, ordinarily low-risk aspects of the business were being done. Bank servicers, including the law firms and other vendors they employed, were skipping steps in

back-office operations and mismanaging case files in systemic dimensions.

In retrospect, everyone should have realized the dangers lurking in the unprecedented volume of foreclosures being processed. Without question, regulatory agencies, including the OCC, should have caught this sooner.

However, once the problem came to light, we set to work immediately. We directed our banks to conduct self-assessments while we prepared to launch an intensive set of "horizontal" examinations that would look at these issues across a field of 14 large servicers across the system. Our examiners then documented the seriousness of those problems.

While all of the loans in the sample we looked at were seriously delinquent, we also uncovered critical deficiencies and shortcomings that constituted unsafe and unsound banking practices, and that resulted in violations of various laws and rules. Along with the Federal Reserve and the OTS, we took enforcement actions, entering into orders with each of the servicers aimed at fixing what was broken, compensating borrowers who were harmed, and ensuring a fair and orderly foreclosure process going forward. With the transition of the OTS into the OCC, we are now responsible for 12 of the 14 servicers.

This is a huge undertaking, and it will take a year and more to bring it to a conclusion. To illustrate its scope, the servicers estimate that as many as 4.5 million borrowers and former homeowners could potentially seek a review of their cases. We have directed the servicers to use sampling techniques to evaluate these portfolios of borrowers, but more importantly, we have also put in place a process that will allow any borrower who believes he or she was financially harmed by the unsafe and unsound practices addressed in the orders to request an independent review of his or her case. As a result of these reviews, identified financial harm will be remedied for such borrowers.

This is only one of the many important issues we are dealing with, but it may be the most important. Getting the real estate sector back on its feet is one of the keys to economic recovery, and solving the foreclosure problem in a way that ensures fair treatment of America's families is necessary to reestablish trust in our financial system.

It is unfortunately true that significant numbers of homeowners continue to face the loss of

their homes in our slow-growth economy, but it must also be true that troubled borrowers can expect to be treated fairly. I am confident that our enforcement actions will do just that: ensure that at-risk borrowers get a fair chance to stay in their homes, while assuring that those who do find themselves in foreclosure receive appropriate protection and due process of law.

The challenges ahead are significant, but the U.S. economy will not be restored to full prosperity without a strong banking system. An economy as large as ours needs large banks to finance it, but it also depends on the diversity and personalized service provided by small and midsize banks. Such diversity has long characterized our banking system, and that is unlikely to change since economic systems naturally organize in this way.

Federally chartered institutions, operating under uniform national standards, are a critical part of that system. We at the OCC have worked hard over the last year to

restore and ensure the viability of the institutions we supervise, aiming to make that system

- a safe system that manages risk and maintains ample liquidity and strong capital;
- a sound system that provides innovative service to businesses and individuals, complies with applicable laws, and earns a reasonable profit; and
- a well-managed system that is efficient and responsive to the needs of the communities it serves.

What remains is for the banks and federal savings associations that make up the federal system to put the lingering effects of the financial crisis behind them and restore the trust and confidence of the American people. Our goal is to make that happen.

John Walsh

John Walsh
Acting Comptroller
of the Currency

With the addition of hundreds of former OTS employees with extensive experience as regulators of mortgage lenders, the OCC was significantly enhanced in numbers and know-how as it helped confront the nation's ongoing housing difficulties in 2011.

Section One
Year in Review—Housing in the Forefront

Introduction

In fiscal year 2011,[2] the U.S. financial system continued the process of recovery from the economic crisis of 2007 to 2009 while undergoing some of the most sweeping regulatory changes since the Great Depression.

The year was characterized by extreme economic volatility. During the first half, most indicators were positive. Rising corporate profits bolstered investor confidence, sending stock markets broadly higher. As the year wore on, however, the recovery faltered, as persistent high unemployment, rising energy prices, weak consumer spending, and rising public sector debt, both at home and abroad, took their toll.

The persistent weakness in residential real estate markets has slowed the economic recovery. Although home-price declines moderated in most U.S. markets in 2011, the drop in values still left millions of Americans—nearly one in five—owing more than their homes were worth. Homeowners were unable to sell, refinance to take advantage of lower interest rates, or move in search of better jobs. The slumping residential real estate market hurt

the construction-related industries. That in turn weakened banks with the greatest exposures to loan losses in those industries.

Despite the challenging economic environment, the condition and profitability of the national banking industry, supervised by the OCC, improved during 2011. National banks of all sizes, in aggregate, experienced improvements in earnings, asset quality, balance sheet liquidity, and capital. The number of banks with the most serious safety and soundness issues declined for the first time since 2006.

Notwithstanding these positive signs, the level of problem loans that banks must work through remained elevated and continues to require close attention by bank management and supervisors. Persistent weaknesses in commercial and residential real estate markets posed significant challenges for banks with concentrations in these markets. Losses from these exposures continued to be a key factor in the majority of bank failures in 2011: During the 12-month period, a total of 104 banks and federal savings associations, also known as thrifts, failed. Of these, 15 were national banks and nine were federal savings associations.

Implementation of the landmark Dodd–Frank Act was the most

important regulatory development of the year. Dodd–Frank required the OCC and other federal financial regulatory agencies to write hundreds of new regulations and conduct multiple studies that touched on every facet of the financial services industry.

Dodd–Frank also brought important changes to the structure of financial regulation. The act created a new regulatory agency, the CFPB, to regulate the provision of consumer financial products and services, including residential mortgages, across the financial sector. Dodd–Frank eliminated a regulatory agency when it transferred the functions and assets of the OTS to the OCC. Since its creation in 1989, the OTS had served as the regulator of thrifts— the institutions that had long been responsible for most of the nation's mortgage lending. On July 21, 2011, the OCC became the regulator for the more than 600 federal savings associations. The transfer brought to the OCC hundreds of former OTS employees with

---

[2] Unless otherwise noted, all references to 2011 refer to the fiscal year beginning October 1, 2010, and ending September 30, 2011.

Acting Comptroller John Walsh (second from right) testifies before a congressional subcommittee investigating mortgage foreclosure practices.

extensive experience as regulators of mortgage lenders. The OCC was thus significantly enhanced in numbers and know-how as it helped confront the nation's ongoing housing difficulties in 2011.

This *Annual Report FY 2011* focuses on four major themes:

- Addressing problems in the nation's mortgage markets
- Implementing the provisions of Dodd–Frank
- Ensuring the safety and soundness of national banks and federal savings associations
- Enforcing compliance with consumer protection laws and regulations

Addressing Problems in the Nation's Mortgage Markets

Responding to Foreclosure Documentation Problems

The OCC has taken a leadership role in addressing and seeking corrective measures to deficiencies in foreclosure practices that came to light in September 2010. In October 2010, the OCC ordered the eight largest national bank servicers to conduct comprehensive self-assessments of their foreclosure practices. The OCC demanded prompt action for deficiencies, including, when necessary, re-filing documentation with local courts, correcting weaknesses, and bolstering overall governance of the foreclosure process.[3]

At the same time, the OCC initiated planning for a coordinated horizontal review of 14 large mortgage servicers' foreclosure processes with the Federal Reserve Board, the FDIC, and the OTS. More than 100 OCC examiners participated in this effort during the fourth quarter of the 2010 calendar year. They reviewed individual foreclosure case files; tested the validity of servicers' self-assessments and confirmed whether corrective action was taken; determined whether servicers considered alternatives (such as loan modifications) for

troubled borrowers; evaluated the accuracy of servicers' documents and whether the documents were appropriately reviewed; and assessed whether necessary documents to support legal foreclosure proceedings were provided.[4]

During those reviews, examiners found widespread deficiencies and unsafe and unsound practices. These practices, documented in a report published jointly with the Federal Reserve and OTS, provided the basis for strong comprehensive regulatory action taken in April 2011 against the 14 servicers.

The OCC's 2011 consent orders, taken against the eight national bank servicers and two third-party service providers, require servicers to correct deficiencies regarding compliance, oversight of third parties, management information systems, risk management, and communication with borrowers. They require the establishment of a single point of contact for borrowers and the elimination of dual tracking of mortgages when approved for a trial or permanent modification. Most significantly, the orders require servicers to retain independent consultants to conduct a comprehensive "look back" review of foreclosure actions in process in 2009 and 2010 to determine if errors, misrepresentations, or other deficiencies in the process resulted in financial injury to the borrower. In that independent foreclosure review, the OCC and other federal regulators required servicers to establish

[3] Testimony of John Walsh, Acting Comptroller of the Currency, Subcommittee on Housing and Community Opportunity, Committee on Financial Services, U.S. House of Representatives, November 18, 2010, www.occ.gov. All citations in this report's footnotes that refer to the OCC's Web site can be found on either the News and Issuances page or the Publications page.

[4] Testimony of Julie L. Williams, First Senior Deputy Comptroller and Chief Counsel, Committee on the Judiciary, U.S. House of Representatives, December 2, 2010, www.occ.gov.

a process for eligible borrowers to request a review of their cases, if they think they were financially harmed by improper foreclosure practices. Where financial injury is found, the orders require the servicers to remediate that harm.[5]

These foreclosure actions "fix what is broken, identify and compensate borrowers who suffered financial harm, and ensure a fair and orderly mortgage servicing process going forward," said Acting Comptroller of the Currency John Walsh.[6]

The independent foreclosure review began in November 2011 and is expected to take several months to complete.

In addition to the joint review and enforcement actions involving the largest mortgage servicers, in June 2011 the OCC directed all other national banks to conduct self-assessments of their mortgage servicing practices. The agency issued supervisory guidance on foreclosure practices applicable to all mortgage servicers under OCC supervision—guidance that emphasized the importance of improved accountability, third-party oversight, and reliable information systems.[7] The OCC issued a similar directive to all federal savings associations in August

The "OCC Mortgage Metrics Report," prepared quarterly by agency staff, provides valuable data on the performance of U.S. residential mortgages.

2011, after the transfer of the OTS to the OCC.

Homeowners "have the right to expect transparency, accessibility, and fairness from the companies that service their mortgages, and never more than when a borrower is experiencing financial difficulty," Mr. Walsh said in a speech to the professional association Women in Housing and Finance. "Anything less is unacceptable."[8]

Mortgage Metrics

The "OCC Mortgage Metrics Report" is a quarterly publication that, since its debut in June 2008, has provided standardized performance measures for mortgage loans serviced by national banks and federal savings associations. The report quickly became a key tool for bank regulators, lawmakers, and industry analysts seeking a better understanding of home mortgage performance, foreclosure trends, and the effectiveness of loan modifications.

In 2011, the OCC added data organized by state to the report, allowing for a more granular analysis of performance trends, as well as data on the performance of loans held in bank portfolios.

At the end of September 2011, the OCC published its most recent report, covering mortgage performance through the end of the second quarter. The report covered about 63 percent of all first-lien mortgages in the United States, worth $5.7 trillion in outstanding balances.[9] The data showed that mortgage performance overall had improved from a year earlier but declined slightly from the previous quarter, reflecting seasonal effects, high unemployment, and a slow economic recovery.

The report also showed that servicers continued to process large inventories of delinquent mortgages, with 4 percent of the total portfolio in the process of foreclosure and another 4.9 percent remaining seriously delinquent

[5] Office of the Comptroller of the Currency, "OCC Takes Enforcement Action Against Eight Servicers for Unsafe and Unsound Foreclosure Practices," news release 2011-47, April 13, 2011, www.occ.gov.

[6] Testimony of John Walsh, Acting Comptroller of the Currency, Subcommittee on Housing and Community Opportunity, Committee on Financial Services, U.S. House of Representatives, November 18, 2010, www.occ.gov.

[7] Office of the Comptroller of the Currency, "Foreclosure Management," bulletin 2011-29, June 30, 2011, www.occ.gov.

[8] Remarks by John Walsh, Women in Housing and Finance, April 14, 2011, www.occ.gov.

[9] Office of the Comptroller of the Currency, "OCC Mortgage Metrics Report," Second Quarter 2011, www.occ.gov.

at the end of the quarter.[10] From January 1, 2010, through the second quarter of 2011, servicers implemented nearly 1.1 million modifications, reducing borrowers' monthly principal and interest payments by more than 25 percent on average.[11]

While home retention options—loan modifications, trial-period plans, and payment plans—can help prevent avoidable foreclosures, they will not work in every case, and completed foreclosures will rise as the large number of foreclosures in process continue to work through the system and servicers exhaust alternatives to foreclosure.

Real Estate Appraisal and Evaluation Guidelines

Although lenders focus primarily on borrowers' creditworthiness when they consider applications for mortgage loans, they also look at the value of the property pledged to secure the loan as a secondary source of repayment. Professional, independent appraisals are crucial to determining property values.

Since 1994, when federal financial regulatory agencies last published comprehensive supervisory guidance on real estate appraisal requirements, appraisal practices have changed dramatically. Advances in information technology have made the gathering of market information far easier than before. To cut costs and keep up with the demand for their services

in the busy housing markets of the mid-2000s, appraisers increasingly discontinued physical inspections, relying on automated valuation models and the assumption that housing prices would continue to rise. These practices and assumptions contributed to overly optimistic valuations, easy credit, and many home buyers taking on bigger loans than they could afford. Stronger supervisory oversight was needed to restore the independence and integrity of the appraisal process—an essential ingredient in rebuilding confidence in the nation's housing markets.

In response to these issues, the OCC joined the other federal financial regulatory agencies in publishing revised and updated "Interagency Appraisal and Evaluation Guidelines." The guidelines comprise the agencies' recent issuances on appraisal practices and explain minimum supervisory standards for appraisals, including a requirement that lenders select appraisers based on their competence, experience, and knowledge of relevant markets. The guidelines emphasize that lenders must maintain strong internal controls to ensure reliable appraisals and evaluations.[12]

Section 1472 of Dodd–Frank set forth additional requirements to ensure that the appraisals used to underwrite lending decisions are based on appraisers' best professional and independent judgment. An interim final rule, issued by the Federal Reserve Board in October 2010, prohibits appraiser

coercion, forbids appraisers from having financial interest in transactions, and establishes a procedure for identifying violations of these regulations. The rule went into effect on April 1, 2011.

Credit-Risk Retention

Section 941 of Dodd–Frank charged federal financial regulatory agencies with formulating rules that required lenders to retain a 5 percent interest in any assets not held on their books, while authorizing exemptions for loans with the lowest credit risk, particularly QRMs. But the law left many complicated issues to be resolved by regulation, including the level and structure of risk to be retained and the definition of a QRM. Overlaying these issues is potential concern about how the final rules might affect the cost and availability of credit at a time when mortgage loans are already hard to acquire for many borrowers.

---

[10] Office of the Comptroller of the Currency, "OCC Mortgage Metrics Report," Second Quarter 2011, table 7, www.occ.gov.

[11] Office of the Comptroller of the Currency, "OCC Mortgage Metrics Report," Second Quarter 2011, tables 2 and 24, www.occ.gov.

[12] Office of the Comptroller of the Currency, et al., "Interagency Appraisal and Evaluation Guidelines," December 2, 2010, www.occ.gov.

In interagency discussions leading up to the proposed rules, the OCC emphasized several key principles.

First, the rules had to provide sufficient flexibility to allow the securitization markets to function in a manner that both facilitates the flow of credit to consumers and investors and protects investors. To that end, the proposed rules released for comment on March 31, 2011, offered firms that securitize assets five possible options for handling risk retention, consistent with the Dodd–Frank goal of restoring confidence in the quality of asset-backed securities.[13]

Second, the rules had to be balanced, setting the bar for QRMs neither too high nor too low. The agencies were intent that the requirement not be taken as a new (and highly restrictive) national mortgage standard but rather as the special case the law intended it to be.[14]

Third, the OCC emphasized that the rules must be uniform among the involved agencies and across the institutions they regulate. The proposals that emerged from interagency deliberations provide a single, straightforward set of federal requirements on securitization—risk retention, structure, and disclosure—that applies to all markets, all products, and all securitizers.

President Obama discusses Dodd–Frank implementation issues with senior administration officials. Acting Comptroller John Walsh is at the far left.

Finally, the OCC believed that careful and extensive public review, which is always essential in the rule-making process, was especially important when the rules under consideration had extensive implications for credit availability. Thus, the agencies actively solicited comment on a host of issues and, when the number of public comments far exceeded expectations, extended the comment deadline from June 2011 to August 2011. The final rules are expected to be released in fiscal year 2012.[15]

Implementing Dodd–Frank

Integrating the OCC and the OTS

On July 21, 2011, a key provision of Dodd–Frank was fulfilled when most of the OTS's assets and personnel officially transferred to the OCC and federal thrifts were brought under OCC regulation and supervision. The OTS integration was the culmination of months of intensive effort to unify rules, systems, and processes to ensure a timely and seamless transition for OTS employees and OTS-supervised institutions.[16]

To accomplish these goals, Senior Deputy Comptroller and Chief Financial Officer Thomas R. Bloom led an OCC working group that collaborated with counterparts from the OTS, the Federal Reserve (which became responsible for the holding companies of thrifts), and the FDIC (which assumed supervisory responsibility for state-chartered thrifts). In January 2011, the agencies delivered to Congress a "Joint Implementation Plan" spelling out how the agencies would accomplish the job. The plan was updated in April 2011.[17]

---

[13] Office of the Comptroller of the Currency, et al., "Credit Risk Retention," proposed rule, March 31, 2011, www.occ.gov.

[14] Statement of John Walsh, Federal Deposit Insurance Corporation Board of Directors, March 29, 2011, www.occ.gov.

[15] Testimony of Julie L. Williams, Subcommittee on Capital Markets and Government Sponsored Entities, Financial Services Committee, U.S. House of Representatives, April 14, 2011, www.occ.gov; Office of the Comptroller of the Currency, et al., "Credit Risk Retention," proposed rule, June 7, 2011, www.occ.gov.

[16] See "Records Integration and Freedom of Information Act" and "Policy Integration Project" in the "OCC Profiles" section of this report for a more detailed look at how the two agencies dealt with some of the challenges of reconciling infrastructure and back-office functions.

[17] Board of Governors of the Federal Reserve System, et al., "Joint Implementation Plan, 301-326 of the Dodd–Frank Wall Street Reform and Consumer Protection Act," January 2011 (revised April 2011), www.occ.gov.

OCC and OTS examiners collaborate to promote effective supervision of national banks and federal savings associations.

The OCC launched an extensive internal communication campaign to smooth the integration of the two agencies, which, while previously operating under different statutory regimes, had similar missions but varying policies and procedures. Automated bulletin boards allowed for the exchange of questions and answers, and group events gave the OTS and OCC staffs opportunities to meet. Like the majority of OCC examiners, most OTS employees would work in the OCC's Midsize and Community Bank Supervision Department. Over many months, Senior Deputy Comptroller Jennifer C. Kelly, the OCC executive in charge of that department, and her team prepared the groundwork for the transition and conducted a series of meetings and conference calls with OTS employees to explain, among other things, how the OCC intended to use and develop their skills.

Under the leadership of Timothy T. Ward, a veteran OTS executive whom the OCC had named Deputy Comptroller for Thrift

Supervision,[18] the agencies developed a staffing plan that integrated the supervision of thrifts into the existing OCC structure, developed examination plans and supervisory strategies for former OTS-supervised institutions, and created a number of new management positions. The plan, which was tested in a series of pilot examinations in the OCC's Central District between January 2011 and April 2011, called for OTS and OCC examiners to be deployed without regard to whether the institution in question was a national bank or a thrift. The pilot helped the agencies identify and address conflicts and gaps in examination documentation procedures, training and certification, and automated supervisory systems.

The pilot examination program also provided federally chartered thrifts with a greater understanding of the OCC's approach to supervision. Related initiatives included publishing a brochure titled "The OCC's Approach to Supervision" and a series of letters to thrift institutions from Acting Comptroller Walsh that provided updates on the integration process.[19] The agency also held a series of 17 informational seminars with executives of thrifts around the country,

which provided an opportunity, as Northeastern District Deputy Comptroller Toney M. Bland told one group, "to establish and encourage ongoing two-way communication, address your concerns, and give you our commitment to provide value-added supervision."[20]

To make the changes necessary to bring regulations into conformity with Dodd–Frank, integrate rules on similar topics, and implement other needed revisions, on July 20, 2011, the OCC issued a final rule implementing several provisions of the Dodd–Frank Act. Provisions included changes to facilitate the transfer of functions from the OTS and revisions to the OCC's rules on preemption and visitorial powers. The revised rules

- eliminated preemption for operating subsidiaries of national banks and operating subsidiaries of federal thrift institutions.
- applied to federal thrifts the same preemption standard—that is, a conflict preemption

Timothy T. Ward, the OCC's Deputy Comptroller for Thrift Supervision, and a thrift executive discuss the agency's supervisory approach.

[18] Dodd–Frank created the position of Deputy Comptroller for Thrift Supervision.

[19] See "Outreach to Thrifts" in the "OCC Profiles" section of this report.

[20] See "Outreach to Thrifts" in the "OCC Profiles" section of this report.

standard and not an occupation of the field standard—as applies to national banks, and applied to federal thrifts the visitorial powers standard applicable to national banks.

- eliminated ambiguity concerning the preemption standards in OCC regulations by removing language from OCC rules that provides that state laws that "obstruct, impair, or condition" a national bank's powers are preempted.

- revised the OCC's visitorial powers rule to conform to the Supreme Court's *Cuomo* decision, recognizing the ability of state attorneys general to bring enforcement actions in court to enforce applicable laws against national banks as authorized by such laws.[21]

On July 21, 2011, the OCC became the sole federal regulator of 642 federal savings associations and home to 670 former OTS employees. In addition, the OCC was given the authority to prescribe regulations for all federal savings associations. The OCC will be working to integrate sets of rules on similar topics and review stand-alone rules for clarity and consistency through 2013.

Creating the CFPB

The transfer date for OTS integration, July 21, 2011, was also the creation date of the CFPB, which was given rule-making authority that was previously the province of other federal regulatory agencies,

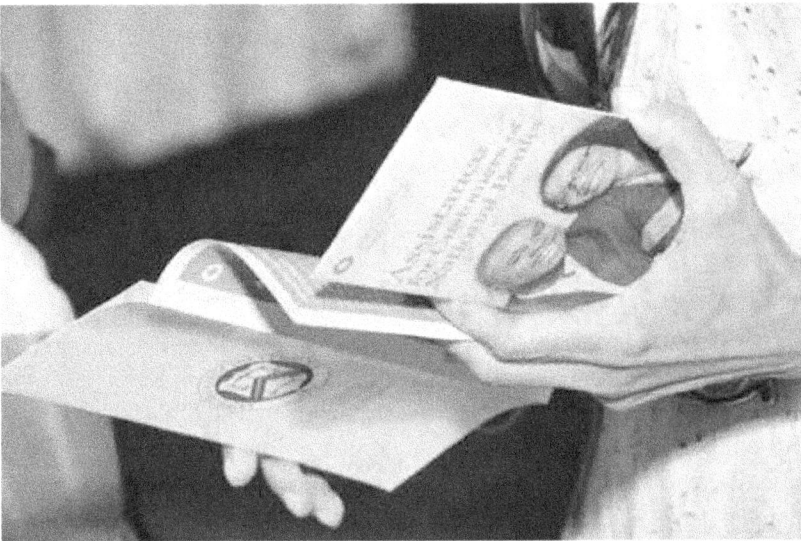

The OCC's publications disseminate valuable information to consumers regarding financial products and services.

such as the OCC, for specified federal consumer financial laws under Dodd–Frank. To ensure compliance with those laws, Dodd–Frank also granted the CFPB authority to supervise banks holding more than $10 billion in assets.

OCC Deputy Comptroller for Large Banks Delora Jee headed an OCC committee that coordinated with the CFPB to ensure a smooth transition. The OCC consulted extensively with CFPB staff on issues ranging from procurement processes to examination techniques, contributing six full-time staff members with diverse and essential institutional expertise.

Congress envisioned that the CFPB would draw staff from the agencies that were transferring responsibilities to it. By agreement with the OCC, the CFPB solicited expressions of interest from OCC employees interested in joining the bureau, in particular those employees working in "transfer-process functions" such as compliance examination, enforcement and

interpretation of consumer financial law, and consumer education. The bureau subsequently made employment offers to individuals who met its needs.[22]

The mission of the OCC's Houston-based Customer Assistance Group, with its sophisticated consumer complaint processing capability, aligns directly with the new bureau's mission.[23] The CFPB will process consumer complaints related to the large financial companies over which it has supervisory authority. The OCC will continue to process questions and complaints concerning consumer issues within the jurisdiction of the OCC through the Customer Assistance Group and will continue to send misdirected complaints it receives to the appropriate federal or

---

[21] Office of the Comptroller of the Currency, "Notice of Proposed Rulemaking," bulletin 2011-20, June 1, 2011, www.occ.gov; "Office of Thrift Supervision Integration; Dodd–Frank Act Implementation," final rule, 76 Fed. Reg. 140 (July 21, 2011), www.gpoaccess.gov.

[22] Consumer Financial Protection Bureau, "Developing Our Human Capital," Annual Report to Congress, July 21, 2011, www.consumerfinance.gov.

[23] For more on the Customer Assistance Group, see the *Annual Report FY 2009*, 44, www.occ.gov.

The Financial Stability Oversight Council addresses systemic risks to the U.S. banking system.

state regulator. In addition, the Customer Assistance Group will process complaints involving national banks and federal savings associations with more than $10 billion in assets on behalf of the CFPB, while the CFPB builds its capacity to handle complaints. Under this approach, the CFPB will begin by handling credit card-related complaints involving national banks and federal savings associations with assets greater than $10 billion and will expand its complaint process to other products and services offered as the new bureau builds that capacity through March 2012.

Financial Stability Oversight Council

Section 111 of Dodd–Frank created the FSOC to assess overall risks to the financial system and coordinate corrective action when systemic risks were identified. The council consists of 10 voting members, one from each of nine federal financial regulatory agencies and an independent member with insurance expertise. On October 1, 2010, Acting Comptroller Walsh represented the OCC at the FSOC's inaugural meeting, presided over by Treasury Secretary Timothy

F. Geithner. The FSOC adopted organizational bylaws and issued a notice of proposed rulemaking bolstering supervision for certain nonbank financial companies. The council also commenced a study of section 619 of Dodd–Frank, the "Volcker rule," which restricts U.S. financial companies from engaging in most kinds of trading using their own funds, otherwise known as proprietary trading.[24]

Rather than create a new permanent bureaucracy at the FSOC, Dodd–Frank envisioned that experts drawn from member agencies would compose the FSOC's committees and working groups. The OCC's Chief National Bank Examiner is a member of the council's deputies' committee, which provides broad oversight and direction on the activities of FSOC's various operating committees. OCC staff members serve on the council's committee on systemic risk and on subcommittees on institutions and markets, which play a major role in the FSOC's analysis of emerging threats to financial stability. The OCC assigned experts to five standing committees that support the FSOC's work in designating

systemically important nonbank financial companies; payment, clearing, and settlement activities; heightened prudential standards; orderly liquidation authority and resolution plans; and data collection and analysis. Additionally, OCC attorneys participated in the FSOC's informal legal staff working group, which provides the council with legal guidance.[25]

Dodd–Frank and Basel III

Capital is the bulwark of the banking business, a bank's backstop against loss and insolvency. In the aftermath of the financial crisis, financial institutions were under heavy pressure to build capital to protect themselves against future downturns. While much of this pressure came from financial markets, regulation and supervision also encouraged, and in some cases required, higher bank capital. In revising capital policy in 2011, regulators were tasked with finding the right balance between ensuring safety and soundness and supporting a healthy level of credit availability.

[24] Testimony of John Walsh, Committee on Banking, Housing, and Urban Affairs, U.S. Senate, February 17, 2011, www.occ.gov.

[25] Testimony of Timothy W. Long, Senior Deputy Comptroller for Bank Supervision Policy and Chief National Bank Examiner, Subcommittee on Oversight and Investigations, Financial Services Committee, U.S. House of Representatives, April 14, 2011, www.occ.gov.

The Basel Committee on Banking Supervision, of which the OCC is a member, brings bank supervisors from around the world together to promote consistent and high-quality supervision. In December 2010, the committee adopted a new international framework focused on strengthening global capital and liquidity requirements for internationally active banks. This framework—known as Basel III—requires increases in both the amount and quality of regulatory capital relative to banks' risks, including a greater reliance on common equity. Basel III requires banks to hold substantially more liquidity in the form of short-term, low-risk assets and to increase their reliance on more stable long-term debt and core deposits. Basel III introduces other significant enhancements designed to ensure that all material risks confronting financial companies—especially risks held in trading portfolios and the risks posed by complex structured financial products that proved to be most problematic during the crisis—are appropriately reflected in regulatory capital requirements. The OCC was active in the development of these enhanced standards.[26]

Dodd–Frank contains provisions that also aim to enhance the capital and liquidity standards of U.S. financial companies. Among them are sections 115(a) and 115(b), which authorize the FSOC to make recommendations to the Federal Reserve on prudential standards

Newly commissioned national bank examiners take the oath of office.

for risk-based capital, leverage limits, and liquidity requirements at systemically important non-bank financial companies. Section 171(b) of Dodd–Frank also deals with risk-based capital, requiring the banking agencies to develop minimum risk-based capital rules, not only for commercial banks but also for nonbank financial companies supervised by the Federal Reserve. Other sections set minimum capital floors for large banks. The final rule, published by the banking agencies on June 28, 2011, implemented this minimum capital requirement.[27]

Although provisions of Dodd–Frank and Basel III share the goal of raising the amount and the quality of bank capital, they differ in important respects, and these differences raise questions that the U.S. federal banking agencies must address as they move forward with implementation. These issues include such questions as, what should count as capital? To which institutions should the standards apply? How much risk is inherent in the various asset classes that

banks hold on their books? How much capital must be held in each instance? In the new fiscal year, U.S. regulators will weigh the costs and benefits of adopting a single set of Basel III-compatible standards for all U.S. banks.[28]

Ensuring Safety and Soundness

As government agencies begin to implement Dodd–Frank, the ultimate impact on the financial institutions that are subject to its new rules and structures will be significant. Given the changing regulatory environment for national banks and federal savings associations, and with the outlook for the economy still uncertain, the OCC's core mission of protecting safety and soundness is more important than ever.[29]

The OCC takes a differentiated approach to its bank supervisory activities, providing supervision tailored to the distinctive needs of national banks and federal savings associations of varying sizes and

[26] Bank for International Settlements, Basel Committee on Banking Supervision, "Basel III: A Global Regulatory Framework for More Resilient Banks and Banking Systems," December 16, 2010 (revised June 2011), www.bis.org.

[27] Testimony of John Walsh, Committee on Banking, Housing, and Urban Affairs, U.S. Senate, February 17, 2011, www.occ.gov.

[28] Remarks by John Walsh, Exchequer Club, January 19, 2011, www.occ.gov.

[29] Remarks by John Walsh, Independent Community Bankers of America, March 23, 2011, www.occ.gov.

levels of complexity. Institutions in the OCC's Large Bank Supervision program have businesses that cover the broadest geographic span and encompass a wide range of financial products and services. Large and midsize banks receive constant monitoring by teams of resident examiners, many of them specialists in such areas as asset management, commercial credit, retail credit, compliance, capital markets, information technology, mortgage banking, and operational risk. This full-time, on-site presence helps bank examiners develop a close understanding of the banks' risk taking and risk management; identify the most significant risks; and determine the adequacy of bank systems and controls to measure, monitor, and manage these risks.

Community-based institutions constitute the vast majority of the more than 2,000 national banks and federal savings associations under the OCC's jurisdiction. These institutions receive risk-based supervision by examiners who are typically members of the communities in which the banks they supervise do business. These examiners have firsthand familiarity with local economic conditions,

while the OCC's national network of field, satellite, and district offices provides insight into larger economic, financial, and regulatory trends that affect banks of all sizes. This combination of local presence and national perspective adds significant value to OCC supervision.

Given the continued weakness in the economic environment, credit risk and credit-risk management continue to be a major focus of OCC supervisory activities in all banks. Examiners pay particular attention to the quality of systems for rating credit risk and identifying problem loans; the adequacy of loan-loss reserves in light of deteriorating credit quality; and the effectiveness of loan work-out strategies. They look for sound policies and structures for managing interest rate risk and liquidity risk, based on diversified funding sources and realistic plans for contingency funding. Recognizing that effective risk management policies require a supportive risk management culture, they evaluate the role of a bank's board of directors and senior managers in promoting those policies. In the case of community banks, examiners emphasize the importance of identifying potential concentrations in key portfolios, such as commercial real estate, to identify problems before they surface. The OCC's findings are communicated directly to the bank's leaders.

Guidance on Model Risk Management

In recent years, the largest, most complex national banks have placed increasing reliance on sophisticated quantitative models to conduct many parts of their business. And the use of models is not limited to the largest banks; banks of all sizes use models to manage risk, price products, and make many fundamental business decisions.

The OCC recognizes the benefits that such models provide. The OCC has long emphasized, however, that the use of models also carries risk, and the potential for model-related financial loss, reputational damage, or poor decisions must be managed as a risk, just as any other source of risk would be addressed within banks' overall risk-management structures.

These key principles are reflected in "Supervisory Guidance on Model Risk Management," which was released by the OCC and the Federal Reserve in April 2011. The guidance, which builds on the OCC's 2000 guidance on model validation, articulates the elements of a sound program for managing model risk and provides guidance to OCC examiners and the banks they supervise on prudent model risk-management policies, procedures, practices, and standards.[30]

Stress Testing

Beginning in February 2009, in connection with the Supervisory Capital Assessment Program, the

---

[30] Office of the Comptroller of the Currency, "Supervisory Guidance on Model Risk Management," bulletin 2011-12, April 4, 2011, www.occ.gov.

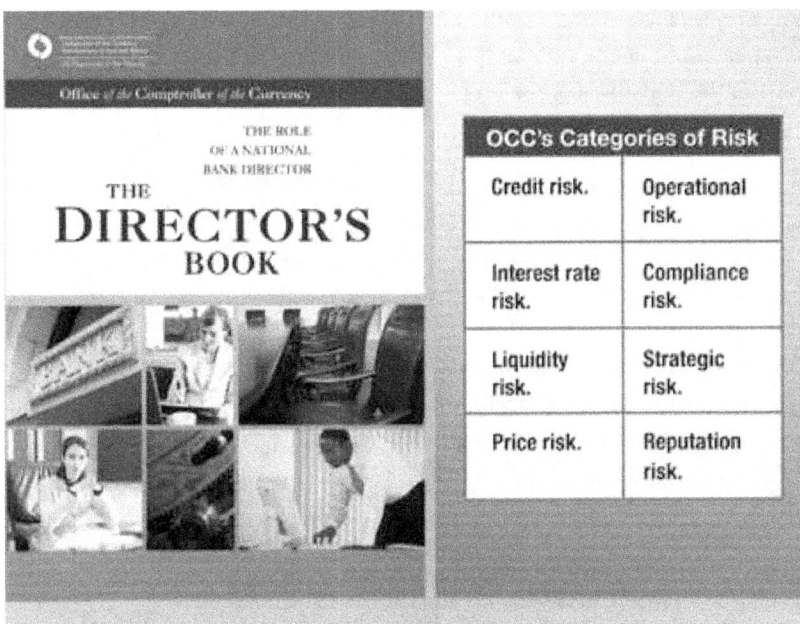

OCC's Categories of Risk	
Credit risk.	Operational risk.
Interest rate risk.	Compliance risk.
Liquidity risk.	Strategic risk.
Price risk.	Reputation risk.

OCC and the Federal Reserve worked with 19 large bank holding companies to carry out stress tests that assessed the ability of these companies to absorb significantly worse than expected losses and still continue to provide credit to the economy. The stress testing program was widely viewed as a turning point in resolving the financial crisis.[31] Regulators learned much from that experience, which highlighted the value of regularly conducting rigorous, credible tests to assess the potential impact of stressful economic events on the financial condition of banks.

In June 2011, the OCC, the FDIC, and the Federal Reserve released for comment guidance that provides an overview of how large banking organizations should develop a structure for stress-testing programs and why such programs are crucial for managing credit risk and liquidity risk. The proposed guidance also cites the importance of strong internal governance and controls in an effective stress-testing framework.[32] The OCC continues to coordinate with the Federal Reserve on implementing stress-testing requirements under section 165(i) of Dodd–Frank.

Derivatives Trading and Guidance on Counterparty Risk Management

After a steep multiyear decline, the market for derivatives rebounded in 2011, as large banks and their customers sought to hedge against risks and market volatility. The derivatives market is the province of large banks: The five largest commercial banks held 96 percent of the total notional amount of derivatives contracts, and the top 25 banks held 100 percent.[33]

Interagency guidance on counterparty credit-risk management, released in July 2011, addressed weaknesses in the management of these risks, which became apparent during the financial crisis.[34] These weaknesses included shortcomings in the timeliness and accuracy of assessing banks' aggregate exposures to a counterparty and inadequate measures of correlation risks across counterparties. The interagency guidance addressed these weaknesses by emphasizing prudent oversight by banks' boards of directors and senior managers and by developing metrics to measure counterparty exposure and the likelihood of deterioration or default.

Survey of Credit Underwriting Practices

In June 2011, the OCC released its 17th annual survey of trends in lending standards and credit risk for the most common types of commercial and retail credit offered by national banks. The "2011 Survey of Credit Underwriting Practices" highlighted how various factors, such as competition among financial providers and the performance of the broader economy, affect the way banks price and underwrite loans, and whether the OCC

---

[31] Office of the Comptroller of the Currency, *Annual Report FY 2009*, 11–12, www.occ.gov.

[32] Office of the Comptroller of the Currency, "Agencies Seek Comment on Stress Testing Guidance," news release 2011-67, June 9, 2011, www.occ.gov.

[33] Office of the Comptroller of the Currency, "OCC Reports Second Quarter Trading Revenue of $7.4 Billion," news release 2011-118, September 16, 2011, www.occ.gov.

[34] Office of the Comptroller of the Currency, "Agencies Issue Guidance on Counterparty Credit Risk Management," news release 2011-88, July 5, 2011, www.occ.gov.

believes that the inherent credit risk in bank portfolios is increasing or decreasing.[35]

The 2011 survey included examiner assessments of credit underwriting standards at 54 of the largest national banks—those with assets of $3 billion or more. The survey encompassed loans as of December 31, 2010, totaling $4.2 trillion, or 94 percent of total loans in the national banking system at the time.

The 2011 survey contained positive news. A majority of examiners surveyed said credit risk embedded in bank portfolios was stable or improving. Examiners reported easing of underwriting standards for most types of loans to businesses, as banks responded to intensified competition and took advantage of more readily available funding to gain new customers and market share.

The retail portion of the market, however, was a different story. Most of the national banks surveyed were still working through losses sustained on credit cards, home equity loans, and residential

real estate. That residue, combined with persistent unemployment, woes in the housing market, and uncertainties in the consumer economy, led most banks to maintain, or even tighten, credit underwriting standards.

In short, the 2011 survey revealed an industry still recovering from the financial crisis but making significant strides toward regaining its confidence and capacity to support U.S. business and consumers through prudent lending.

While the easing of underwriting standards is normal and a healthy sign of economic stabilization, the OCC warned national banks that the pace of eased standards for certain loan products, most notably leveraged loans, was disconcerting and warranted closer attention by bankers. The OCC carefully monitors the institutions under its supervision to ensure that appropriate underwriting standards are maintained as lending activity continues to revive.

Shared National Credit Program

A similar picture of an industry in transition emerged in the annual Shared National Credit Program review, which the OCC conducts with the Federal Reserve and the FDIC. A shared national credit is any loan of $20 million or more that is shared by three or more federally supervised institutions. The program began in 1977 to promote consistent analysis of shared national credits. The 2011 review covered $910 billion, nearly a third of all such credits in the shared national credit portfolio.

A substantial backlog of poorly underwritten loans, mostly from 2006 and 2007, continued to dampen the outlook for the shared national credits portfolio. Indeed, almost 60 percent of the criticized assets (loans rated "special mention," substandard, doubtful, or loss) originated in those two years. The fact that shared national credits were up only negligibly—less than 1 percent—from the year before reflected the slow recovery of the U.S. economy.

Nonetheless, the overall credit quality of the reviewed loans improved in 2011 for the second year in a row. Loans rated as doubtful or loss, the two weakest categories, fell by 50 percent to $24 billion. Classified assets declined 30 percent, representing 9 percent of the total portfolio, compared with 12 percent in 2010.[36]

Incentive-Based Compensation Practices

Section 956 of Dodd–Frank requires federal financial regulatory agencies to regulate incentive compensation arrangements at the financial institutions under their supervision. Specifically, the law instructs the agencies to prohibit incentive-based payment arrangements that provide "excessive compensation or could lead to material financial loss" for financial institutions.

Accordingly, in March 2011, the agencies issued a proposed rule that required banks to identify and

---

[35] Office of the Comptroller of the Currency, "2011 Survey of Credit Underwriting Practices," www.occ.gov; Board of Governors of the Federal Reserve System and Office of the Comptroller of the Currency, "Supervisory Guidance on Model Risk Management," April 4, 2011, www.occ.gov.

[36] Board of Governors of the Federal Reserve System, Federal Deposit Insurance Corporation, and Office of the Comptroller of the Currency, "Shared National Credits Program, 2011 Review," August 2011, www.occ.gov.

Consumer Advisories and Public Service Announcements

The OCC issued two consumer advisories in 2011 that were widely publicized through OCC public service announcements.

For families in danger of losing their homes, the threat of foreclosure can engender fear and desperation. Unscrupulous criminals view such situations as opportunities to prey on vulnerable homeowners. Scam tactics vary, as the OCC's consumer advisory titled "Avoiding Mortgage Modification Scams and Foreclosure Rescue Scams" points out.

The culprits might ask for a large up-front cash payment—always a red flag—to negotiate a settlement with lenders. They might encourage troubled borrowers to file for bankruptcy, or stop communicating with lenders, or take advantage of an imaginary government assistance program, or, perhaps worst of all, sign over their property to a third-party, with the promise of more affordable financing to come. Do that, the OCC warns, and the next step could be an eviction notice.

How can a consumer avoid these traps? Awareness is the first step. The OCC's public service announcement describes false promises and enticements that should make people in need of mortgage assistance run in the opposite direction. What they should do instead, the OCC advises, is to call a toll-free number that provides access to a housing counselor approved by the

U.S. Department of Housing and Urban Development. The advice is free, and there are no strings attached.[37]

As technology evolves and adapts, so do the criminals who try to exploit it.

As another OCC consumer advisory explains, one of the latest and most sophisticated frauds is card skimming—tampering with automated teller machines (ATM) or other cash machines to steal information that criminals can use to loot bank accounts.

In card skimming, a bank customer makes a routine ATM deposit or withdrawal and does not notice that a "skimmer," which reads and transmits card information, is installed on the ATM. Sometimes a remote camera is installed, too, enabling criminals to record keystrokes and steal customers' pass codes. Often, customers only discover tampering when their bank accounts have been wiped out.

The consumer advisory offers tips on how to avoid skimming. These include walking away from an ATM if someone is watching nearby; checking the card slot to be sure it is an integral part of the cash machine; and examining card statements for unauthorized withdrawals and immediately reporting anything suspicious to the financial institution.[38]

In personal finance, as in so many aspects of people's lives, technology brings benefits. But using it safely requires vigilance.

---

[37] Office of the Comptroller of the Currency, "Avoiding Mortgage Modification Scams and Foreclosure Rescue Scams," consumer advisory 2011-1, February 24, 2011, www.occ.gov.

[38] Office of the Comptroller of the Currency, "Avoiding 'Card Skimming' at ATMs and Other Money Machines," consumer advisory 2011-2, June 1, 2011, www.occ.gov.

eliminate incentive compensation arrangements that encouraged inappropriate risks and risk taking by their employees. The proposed rule required institutions with more than $1 billion in assets to implement formal policies and procedures governing incentive compensation arrangements and to submit an annual report to their federal regulator describing that structure. Larger institutions (with more than $50 billion in assets) would have to defer at least 50 percent of the incentive compensation of certain bank officers for three years, with the ultimate payment adjusted to reflect any losses.[39]

Internet Authentication Practices

In October 2005, the federal banking agencies issued guidance titled "Authentication in an Internet Banking Environment," which discussed risk management expectations regarding fraud prevention and safeguarding customer information. Since that time, online threats to financial institutions and their customers have grown in size and sophistication. Therefore, in June 2011, the agencies released supplemental guidance to reinforce the risk management framework and update their expectations regarding customer authentication, layered security, and other controls in an increasingly hostile online environment.

The supplemental guidance requires banks to perform periodic risk assessments of their controls,

assessing new and evolving threats to the security of online accounts and taking the necessary steps to strengthen and enhance those controls. OCC examiners will continue to assess the adequacy of banks' controls, including any remediation plans, as part of their ongoing supervision and the enhanced expectations outlined in the supplementary guidance.[40]

Enforcing Compliance With Consumer Protection Laws and Regulations

The OCC is dedicated to protecting consumers and enforcing consumer protection laws. Although Dodd–Frank transferred authority to the CFPB for supervising most areas of consumer compliance at banks and federal savings associations with more than $10 billion in assets, the OCC retains exclusive authority to supervise for compliance with the Bank Secrecy Act, the Community Reinvestment Act, and flood insurance rules, among other regulations. The OCC continues to provide comprehensive compliance supervision at the more than 1,900 community banks and federal savings associations under its jurisdiction.

It is the OCC's unwavering commitment that all bank customers should be treated fairly, that they have access to credit and other basic banking services, and that the terms and conditions of the products and services provided by national banks and federal savings

associations are communicated to consumers transparently and honestly.

In 2011, the OCC's examiners, especially compliance specialists, monitored bank products and practices across the industry. When questionable practices at national banks or federal savings associations came to light, bank managers were instructed to correct them. When supervisory intervention proved inadequate, the OCC has not hesitated to take legally binding enforcement action.

In disputes involving consumers and their banks, the OCC's Customer Assistance Group, which operates under the agency's independent Office of the Ombudsman, is an important resource. Between 2006 and 2010, the Customer Assistance Group processed nearly 150,000 written complaints and fielded 115,000 telephone inquiries, providing consumers with needed information and assistance in dispute resolution.[41]

The OCC communicates directly with consumers by issuing consumer advisories and public service announcements, which appear in local newspapers and other media. And the agency conducts an extensive bilingual outreach program, using Spanish-language multimedia and print publications to bring vital information to consumers' attention and help them make wise financial decisions.

---

[39] Office of the Comptroller of the Currency, "Agencies Seek Comment on Proposed Rule on Incentive Compensation," news release 2011-37, March 30, 2011, www.occ.gov.

[40] Office of the Comptroller of the Currency, "Authentication in an Internet Banking Environment," bulletin 2011-26, June 28, 2011, www.occ.gov.

[41] Office of the Comptroller of the Currency, "Report From the Office of the Ombudsman, 2006–2010 Highlights," June 2011, www.occ.gov.

Supervisory Guidance on Prepaid Access Programs

Prepaid access devices, which enable consumers to handle their money electronically, are among the fastest growing segments of the payment sector. These devices, which include reloadable cards, payroll cards, government benefit cards, retail gift cards, mobile phones with banking applications, and Web sites, allow consumers to add, store, spend, and withdraw funds from many sources.

Because prepaid access devices provide anonymous access to funds through electronic channels, criminals can take advantage of them to commit fraud and money laundering. Banks, therefore, must manage these products with extreme care.

New supervisory guidance issued by the OCC encourages national banks to develop and implement comprehensive risk management programs to ensure that prepaid access devices are safe from thieves and terrorists. The guidance cautions banks that entrusting the operation of these devices to unsupervised third parties does not absolve the originating institutions from resulting damages or from responsibility for comprehensive risk management.[42]

Enforcement Actions

The OCC's actions against national banks and third-party service providers in connection with foreclosure processing deficiencies described on page 8 of this report also benefited consumers. A summary of OCC enforcement actions in 2011 is presented on page 41.

In other instances in which the OCC took action to protect consumers from unfair and abusive banking practices, a substantial civil money penalty was imposed on a national bank relating to the marketing and sale of a credit protection product by its auto finance subsidiary. The OCC found that this practice involved materially false, deceptive, or otherwise misleading practices in violation of the Federal Trade Commission Act.[43]

Another case involved a national bank whose new customers were automatically enrolled in its overdraft program 30 days after opening their accounts. Any time an account was overdrawn, a fee was imposed. If the account stayed overdrawn for more than seven days, there was an additional fee. The OCC found that these terms, which made it impossible for some customers to escape from their overdrawn status, were not properly advertised in the bank's brochures.[44]

The OCC imposed a consent order that levied a $1 million civil penalty against the bank and required it to establish a fund of at least $32 million to reimburse consumers who were harmed by practices deemed unfair and deceptive. The OCC also ordered the bank to improve its corporate governance and revamp its overdraft program to ensure that such abuses did not occur again.[45]

---

[42] Office of the Comptroller of the Currency, "OCC Issues Guidance on Prepaid Access," news release 2011-83, June 29, 2011, www.occ. gov; Office of the Comptroller of the Currency, "Prepaid Access Programs: Risk Management Guidance and Sound Practices," bulletin 2011-27, June 28, 2011, www.occ.gov.

[43] Office of the Comptroller of the Currency, "OCC Assesses Civil Money Penalty Against JPMorgan Chase Bank, N.A.," news release 2011-70, June 15, 2011, www.occ.gov.

[44] Office of the Comptroller of the Currency, "In the Matter of Woodforest National Bank: Consent Order for a Civil Money Penalty," October 8, 2010, www.occ.gov.

[45] Office of the Comptroller of the Currency, "Agreement by and Between Woodforest National Bank, The Woodlands, Texas, and The Comptroller of the Currency," October 8, 2010, www.occ.gov.

In fiscal year 2011, the OCC undertook a variety of initiatives to advance its diversity and openness objectives, while promoting access to financial services and effective supervision of the national system of banks and federal savings associations.

Section Two
OCC Profiles

Equal Employment Opportunity and Diversity

Dodd–Frank assigned important responsibilities regarding diversity to the OCC and other financial regulatory agencies and directed each agency to establish an Office of Minority and Women Inclusion (OMWI).

"It is important that the OCC as a government agency reflect the population of our country," says Joyce Cofield, Executive Director of the OCC's OMWI. "The more diverse an organization is, the better opportunity it has to bring in the best and brightest talent."

Diversity has long been an OCC priority for building and sustaining a top-flight workforce. Before passage of Dodd–Frank, OCC leaders had taken steps to combine the OCC's offices on diversity and equal employment opportunity. The framework was already in place to meet the new law's requirement to develop standards for supporting diversity and equal employment opportunity in the OCC workforce and among senior management.

The law goes further, however, requiring the regulatory agencies to set goals for increasing the number of contracts awarded

to minority-owned and women-owned firms and for assessing diversity policies and practices at OCC-regulated institutions. The OCC is working closely with the other federal financial regulatory agencies to develop a common set of standards for these mandates and to coordinate implementation.

Part of the OMWI mission is to promote fair treatment and employee engagement in the OCC workforce. In January 2011, the OCC submitted a program status report to the U.S. Equal Employment Opportunity Commission. The report highlighted the OCC's accomplishments in 2010 and discussed plans for 2011.

The program's goals are to

- implement a system to collect and track diversity-related data on applicants for entry-level bank examiner positions;
- increase participation of Hispanic employees in the OCC workforce;
- increase participation of female bank examiners in the OCC workforce;
- increase participation of employees with disabilities in the OCC workforce;

- increase participation of women and minorities in senior positions in the OCC workforce; and
- increase the use of alternative dispute resolution for addressing equal employment opportunity complaints.

The OCC's National Diversity Internship Program, which began in 2011, provided professional career experience for select minority and female college students, while reaffirming the OCC's commitment to an expert, highly motivated, and diverse workforce. Twelve interns, working out of OCC Headquarters in Washington, served in a variety of capacities in 2011; in 2012, the program will expand to include the OCC's district offices.

OCC employees can become members of five employee diversity or "networking" groups. The Network of Asian Pacific Americans (NAPA), the Hispanic Organization for Leadership and Advancement (HOLA), the Coalition of African-American Regulatory Employees (CARE), the Women's Network, and the Gay, Lesbian, and Straight Alliance (GLSA) provide employees with valued opportunities to build networks, promote professional growth, and advance career progress at the OCC.

All agency employees are required to support the OCC's diversity and equal employment opportunity goals. Moreover, each OCC manager's annual performance evaluation includes a specific requirement to meet such goals, which means that no OCC manager is eligible for the highest overall performance rating without having achieved the highest rating on equal employment opportunity.

Records Integration and Freedom of Information Act

One of the biggest challenges facing the OTS and the OCC when they combined forces was integrating records and records management systems. At OTS Headquarters, records on film and paper were kept in storerooms, file rooms, and individual employees' offices. The OTS regional offices had their own paper records and systems. Fortunately, the OTS also had a comprehensive, well-organized schedule that classified records and their disposition, as well as a dedicated staff of records management professionals.

The OCC records management staff continues to identify OTS records that need to be turned over to the FDIC, which took over regulatory functions for state-chartered savings associations, and to the Federal Reserve, which now regulates former savings and loan holding companies.

Public records under the federal Freedom of Information and Privacy acts also required integration. By the end of 2011, the OCC had realigned its staff to respond to requests for records related to national banks and federal savings associations. As the agency has done for its own records, the OCC digitized the OTS's records, which now can be tracked, processed, and released electronically.

"This system allows us to make an increasing number of documents available to the public—and more efficiently, with less reliance on paper records," says Frank Vance,

the OCC's Manager for Disclosure Services. "This means that the OCC can respond better, faster to customers' needs, especially when the demand for information is on the rise."

Minority-Owned Depository Institutions

Minority-owned national banks and federal savings associations play essential roles in providing financial services to families and small businesses in underserved communities around the country.

Both the OCC and the OTS have long demonstrated a commitment to preserving minority-owned institutions and fostering new ones. The agencies have provided technical assistance, training, and other support to these institutions, which are operated by African-Americans, Asians, Hispanics, Native Americans, and women. That commitment continued unabated under the auspices of the External Outreach and Minority Affairs unit after the OCC and the OTS integration.

At the Interagency Minority-Owned Depository Institution Conference in New York in

June 2011, Acting Comptroller Walsh announced the formation of an advisory committee with representatives of minority-owned national banks and federal savings associations. Mr. Walsh said he expected the committee to provide the OCC with valuable perspectives and insights. "Our goal has to be the preservation of vibrant minority national banks and federal thrifts that are safe, sound, and strong enough to continue to serve their communities," he said.

Like other community banks, minority-owned institutions typically specialize in relationship banking. Managers of these institutions often know their customers by name, are aware of their credit histories, and understand their business needs.

"When a small business needs a quick decision on a loan, [minority-owned banks] can respond because you know the local market, and you know the character of the men and women who stand behind the business," Mr. Walsh said in his remarks at the conference. "That's something that local companies just can't get from large financial institutions."

Many minority-owned institutions, however, are under significant stress. The financial crisis hit their communities particularly hard, and the number of institutions has declined. Those pressures make the continued commitment of the OCC particularly important.

To that end, the OCC held several technical-assistance workshops during the interagency conference.

In addition, the agency waives admission fees for directors of minority-owned institutions so they may attend OCC workshops that cover subjects that bank directors need to understand, such as credit risk and compliance risk. The OCC also offers targeted technical assistance for individual institutions on credit analysis, loan underwriting, budgeting, strategic planning, compliance with the Bank Secrecy Act, and other issues. The OCC holds quarterly conference calls for supervisory officials in OCC offices to discuss best practices for supporting minority-owned institutions.

"The OCC's support of financial access, financial education, and outreach activities fulfills an important responsibility to the minority community," says Glenda Cross, the senior adviser for External Outreach and Minority Affairs. "These are ways we ensure that the banking system truly supports the financial needs of all Americans."

Policy Integration Project

In January 2011, the OCC embarked on an ambitious project to integrate the more than 1,000 supervisory policies of the OTS into the OCC's policy framework. The goal is to produce a unified supervisory approach for national banks and federal savings associations.

"We are focused on addressing the policy differences in an orderly and timely manner," says project lead Carolyn DuChene, the OCC's Deputy Comptroller for

Operational Risk. Her approach first calls for culling several hundred policies that can be reconciled without significant complications. The next step is to tackle the complex job of vetting policies that differ significantly, ensuring that the differences are effectively aligned with banking laws applicable to the two distinct types of federal banking charters. Until institutions are notified otherwise, OCC policies continue to apply to national banks and OTS policies to federal savings associations.

The project team is closely coordinating with a parallel project in the OCC Chief Counsel's Office to review legal rules. In fact, much of the integration of supervisory policies depends on the results of this legal review, as the policies are largely based on OCC and former OTS regulations. The results of the projects will be incorporated into training for seasoned examiners and into the curriculum that entry-level bank examiners need to master to become successful commissioned National Bank Examiners.

Although OCC Headquarters oversees the policy integration project, bank examiners, attorneys, and other subject-matter experts throughout the agency provide input to the project team. "They are the 'boots on the ground,'" Ms. DuChene says. "They are the best source of information about what works and what doesn't, and the grass-roots approach is essential to making the project a success."

She cautions that a lot of work still needs to be done before finalizing related policy guidance. The emphasis is to "get the things done that are going to have the biggest impact in the field sooner rather than later, within the constraints of the regulation review process," Ms. DuChene says.

Small-Business Lending

Small businesses account for about half or more of all new jobs in the United States. This makes them a key component of the nation's economy. During the economic downturn, many small businesses laid off employees, reduced inventory, and sold assets. Small-business loans by banks declined from 2008 to 2010. As small-business activity recovers, banks must be prepared to resume providing needed credit.

In 2011, the OCC partnered with the U.S. Small Business Administration, the Export–Import Bank of the United States, and the U.S. Department of Agriculture to highlight federal loan guarantee programs that support small-business lending. Recent laws have made these programs more

user-friendly and more attractive to banks.

The OCC sponsored seminars around the country and conducted a nationwide teleconference to better acquaint bank managers with these programs. Community development newsletters and in-depth "Insights" reports as well as bankers' roundtables offered detailed information about how banks could participate while receiving consideration for qualified investments under the Community Reinvestment Act.

"We are getting the banks energized about using these programs," says Barry Wides, OCC Deputy Comptroller for Community Affairs. "We are part of a broad government effort to get banks involved."

For example, two programs provide federal loan guarantees for banks that make loans to small businesses involved in exporting goods or manufacturing components of goods that are exported. The guarantees shield banks from

some of the risk of losses from loan defaults and allow banks to expand the array of financial products offered to their customers. The programs also aim to create jobs and increase exports by providing working capital to small businesses to finance export sales. More than 97 percent of the U.S. companies that export goods overseas are small businesses with fewer than 500 employees.

Another federal initiative provides funding for state programs to support bank lending to small businesses, which must use the money for purposes that include start-up costs and equipment purchases. As states roll out their programs, the OCC continues to work on the local level to promote the programs among national banks and federal savings associations in those areas.

The OCC plans to continue outreach activities that highlight opportunities for banks to become involved in small-business initiatives. Such outreach may be particularly helpful to financial institutions that received funding from the Treasury Department's Small Business Lending Fund. The capital investments that the Treasury Department made in institutions under the program carry dividend rates that go down as the institution's small-business lending goes up.

The OCC and other federal banking agencies expect Small Business Lending Fund participants to extend credit in a safe and sound manner with prudent risk selection and credit-risk management processes. Each participating institution's board of directors should ensure that its small-business lending policy and activity are consistent with safe and sound credit practices and supportive of the institution's participation in the Small Business Lending Fund program.

Outreach to Thrifts

Before the OCC and OTS integration took place, Bert Otto, the Deputy Comptroller in charge of the OCC's Central District, formed a team to schedule 17 "Meet the OCC" meetings around the country for executive leaders of thrifts supervised by the OTS.

"These outreach meetings proved very beneficial," Mr. Otto says. The sessions addressed the OCC's examination process, the philosophy on and approach toward enforcement actions, OCC expectations, the importance of ongoing communication, and the organizational structure of the agency's field offices.

OCC and OTS officials fielded questions on numerous subjects, including interest rate risk and the supervision of mutual savings associations, and assured the executives that former OTS examiners would continue to serve on their examination teams. The message was, "You will have that contact, and you will have that continuity," Mr. Otto says. "That alleviated some fears."

After the meetings, officials from each of the four OCC districts followed up with executives of larger thrifts in one-on-one sessions to discuss the transition.

Outreach to thrifts began well before these meetings. OCC and OTS employees joined forces at conferences and trade shows across the nation to meet bankers and thrift executives and address their concerns. The OCC posted transition-related news on National BankNet (www.banknet.gov), the OCC's private extranet Web site for bankers, and made BankNet available to thrift executives. In March 2011, the OCC invited directors of thrifts to attend the agency's annual workshops for bank directors and increased by 50 percent the number of workshops scheduled for the 2011 calendar year. Those workshops promoted the continuing education

of directors of national banks and thrifts and provided the OCC with invaluable feedback from participants.

The OCC also expects to derive substantial benefit from the Mutual Savings Association Advisory Committee, which it formed late in 2011. This committee, consisting of 10 industry officers and directors, will help the OCC assess the state of mutual savings associations and advise the OCC on ways to help ensure their continued health and viability.

Profitability measured by return on equity at OCC-supervised banking institutions rose to 7.7 percent for the second quarter, which is above the level of a year earlier but still well below levels of recent history.

Section Three
Condition of the National Banking System

Summary

Earnings at national banks and federal savings associations continued to improve in calendar year 2011 from the low levels posted during the financial crisis. Bank capital showed a notable increase. Provision expenses declined again from year-earlier levels but remained well above pre-crisis levels. Credit quality improved, as net charge-off rates fell for all major loan categories. In contrast, erosion in net interest income drove down pre-provision revenues. With loan demand still weak, the substitution of lower-yielding securities for higher-yielding loans compressed interest margins.

Discussion

Net income at OCC-supervised banking institutions for the first half of calendar year 2011 increased by $10.3 billion compared with the first half of 2010. Profitability measured by return on equity rose to 7.7 percent for the second quarter, which is above the level of a year earlier but still well below levels of recent history.

Funding and lending. Business and retail deposits rose sharply during the financial crisis, as other investments appeared less attractive and savers turned to banks for safety. Businesses in particular have accounted for a significant surge in checkable deposits since 2008. Large banks have been the main recipients of these new deposits, which help hold down their funding costs; this pattern extended into 2011. Should business confidence and investment pick up, or returns on alternative investments rise, banks may experience an outflow of these deposits.

Lending by national banks, as measured by the total value of all types of loans on their books, has been declining since the onset of the recession. Loan growth shows only limited signs of recovery. Through the middle of 2011, lending continued to decline in consumer loans, residential real estate, construction, and commercial real estate. The one area of growth in loans for the system as a whole (other than interbank lending) was lending to commercial and industrial borrowers.

Provisions and credit quality. Credit quality has improved steadily over the past two years. Charge-off rates declined for all major loan categories in the first half of 2011 compared with a year earlier. Loan-loss provisions fell by $40.4 billion in the first half of 2011 compared with a year earlier and are now running about 70 percent below the levels that prevailed at the peak of the financial crisis in 2009.

Despite generally improved credit performance, loss rates have remained high for residential real estate loans, due at least in part to the overhang of foreclosed properties. Moreover, about 20 percent of all first-lien mortgages exceed the current value of the homes financed, with much higher shares in the hardest hit states, including Florida, Arizona, and Nevada.

With so many borrowers owing more than their homes are worth and with high rates of joblessness, even many prime residential mortgages are seeing defaults. These forces make a near-term recovery in residential mortgage loss rates less likely. For commercial real estate loans, charge-off rates have stopped rising, but fundamental performance measures, such as vacancy rates and net operating income, are not expected to improve for another year or so.

Revenues. For all OCC-supervised banking institutions, pre-provision net revenues for the first half of 2011 fell 19.7 percent compared with the same period a year earlier, as net interest income eroded. The weak economy has pressured interest margins, as a surge in deposits was funneled into safe but low-yielding cash and securities rather than loans.

Lending remained weak though June 2011, in part because economic growth has been slower than during past recoveries. Continued deleveraging by consumers also appeared to be constraining loan demand. These developments point to continued slow growth in consumer spending (and borrowing), even if gross domestic product growth improves. Corporate profits have recovered to pre-recession levels, but with many firms accumulating cash, and even medium-size firms now able to access the bond markets, banking institutions have experienced less growth in business lending than they did during earlier recoveries.

Noninterest income also fell in the first half of 2011, compared with a year earlier, the result of a sharp drop in deposit and servicing fees and little growth elsewhere. For some of the largest banking institutions with extensive international operations or significant trading activities, noninterest income held up better, though costs related to residential mortgages weighed on the performance of large real estate lenders.

For smaller banks and federal savings associations, revenue growth has been even more of a concern than at larger institutions. Funding costs for smaller institutions did not benefit as much from the sharp drop in interest rates since 2008, and their pre-provision net

revenues as a percent of assets have shown little growth in the recovery so far.

Capital. Over the past two years, national banking institutions have significantly increased their capital levels and strengthened the quality of that capital. While this improvement has been evident across the board, it is especially notable at the largest institutions. A number of forces combined to spur the improvement in capital at large banks; they included market and supervisory pressure, anticipated changes in regulatory capital requirements, and capital increases related to mergers and acquisitions, in addition to a general need to rebuild capital lost during the financial crisis.

The men and women who lead the OCC play a critical role in ensuring the safety and fairness of our national banking system.

Section Four
OCC Organization

Comptroller of the Currency

John Walsh became Acting Comptroller of the Currency on August 15, 2010.

The Comptroller of the Currency is the chief executive of the OCC, which supervises federally chartered commercial banks, federal savings associations, and federal branches and agencies of foreign banks in the United States. The Comptroller also is a director of the Federal Deposit Insurance Corporation and NeighborWorks America.

Mr. Walsh joined the OCC in October 2005 and previously served as Chief of Staff and Public Affairs.

Before joining the OCC, Mr. Walsh was the Executive Director of the Group of Thirty, a consultative group that focuses on international economic and monetary affairs. He joined the group in 1992 and became Executive Director in 1995. Mr. Walsh served on the U.S. Senate Committee on Banking, Housing, and Urban Affairs from 1986 to 1992 and as an international economist for the Treasury Department from 1984 to 1986. Mr. Walsh also served with the Office of Management and Budget (OMB) as an international program analyst, with the Mutual Broadcasting System, and in the U.S. Peace Corps in Ghana.

Mr. Walsh holds a master's degree in public policy from the John F. Kennedy School of Government at Harvard University (1978) and graduated magna cum laude from the University of Notre Dame in 1973. He lives in Catonsville, Md. He is married with four children.

John Walsh, Acting Comptroller of the Currency

Executive Committee

John Walsh
Acting
Comptroller of the
Currency

Julie L. Williams
First Senior
Deputy
Comptroller and
Chief Counsel

John C. Lyons Jr.
Senior Deputy
Comptroller for
Bank Supervision
Policy and Chief
National Bank
Examiner

Michael L. Brosnan
Senior Deputy
Comptroller
for Large Bank
Supervision

Jennifer C. Kelly
Senior Deputy
Comptroller for
Midsize and
Community Bank
Supervision

Thomas R. Bloom
Senior Deputy
Comptroller for
Management and
Chief Financial
Officer

Mark Levonian
Senior Deputy
Comptroller for
Economics

Chief National Bank Examiner's Office

The Chief National Bank Examiner's Office was headed by Senior Deputy Comptroller for Bank Supervision Policy and Chief National Bank Examiner David K. Wilson in the last three months of the fiscal year. Mr. Wilson agreed to accept one of the agency's most critical positions, Examiner-in-Charge of Citibank, and John C. Lyons Jr. subsequently became Senior Deputy Comptroller for Bank Supervision Policy and Chief National Bank Examiner.

The department focuses on developing supervisory policies and examination procedures and tools in the areas of bank information technology, capital, commercial and retail credit risk, compliance, financial markets, balance sheet and asset management, and operational risk. The department includes the Office of the Chief Accountant, which oversees accounting policy guidance for national banks and federal savings associations, and chairs the OCC's National Risk Committee.

Large Bank Supervision

The Department of Large Bank Supervision is headed by Senior Deputy Comptroller Michael L. Brosnan. The department oversees the supervision of the largest and most complex national banking and thrift companies, as well as foreign-owned U.S. branches and agencies.

Midsize and Community Bank Supervision

Senior Deputy Comptroller Jennifer C. Kelly oversees the Midsize and Community Bank Supervision Department. The department is responsible for the supervision of midsize and community banks, focusing on ensuring sound risk identification and management processes and regulatory compliance.

Chief Counsel

First Senior Deputy Comptroller and Chief Counsel Julie L. Williams supervises the OCC's Law, Licensing, and Community Affairs departments.

The Law Department enforces compliance with banking requirements and securities laws, addresses protection and fair treatment of bank customers through enforcement of consumer laws and regulations, issues opinions on national bank powers and activities, handles OCC litigation matters, provides legislative analysis and technical advice, and develops regulations. The Licensing Department charters national banks and federal savings associations and issues decisions on regulated institution structure and business changes. The Community Affairs Department supports national banks and federal savings associations in their community development activities and the provision of financial services to underserved communities and consumers.

Economics

The Economics Department is headed by Senior Deputy Comptroller Mark Levonian. The department provides economic analysis of national and global economic trends, provides on-site and off-site examination support for bank supervision, contributes to policy development, and conducts original research to support the OCC's mission.

Office of Management

The Office of Management is directed by Thomas R. Bloom, the Senior Deputy Comptroller for Management and Chief Financial Officer. The office administers the OCC's human resources, asset acquisition, travel and staff relocation, physical space, training and development, physical and personnel security, compensation and benefits, and financial management. It also provides the OCC's information technology services.

Chief of Staff and Public Affairs

The Public Affairs Department, which reports to the Chief of Staff, supports the OCC through its communications with the banking industry and its representatives, the news media, Congress, and the public. The department is also responsible for the OCC's internal communications program.

Ombudsman

The Office of the Ombudsman administers the national bank appeals program, the OCC's Customer Assistance Group, and the Enterprise Governance unit.

The office, headed by Larry L. Hattix, reports to the Comptroller of the Currency.

Office of Minority and Women Inclusion

The Office of Minority and Women Inclusion, headed by Executive Director Joyce Cofield, is responsible for developing standards for equal employment opportunity and the racial, ethnic, and gender diversity of the OCC's workforce and senior management. The director of this new office reports to the Comptroller of the Currency.

The OCC is responsible for approving or denying changes in corporate or banking structure, while taking supervisory action against institutions that do not comply with laws and regulations or that otherwise engage in unsound practices.

Section Five
Licensing and Enforcement Measures

Figure 1: Corporate Application Activity, National Banks, FY 2010 and FY 2011

	FY 2010	FY 2011	FY 2011 decisions			
	Applications received		Approved	Conditionally approved[a]	Denied	Total[b]
Branches	812	917	868	2	0	870
Capital/sub-debt	269	224	177	8	0	185
Change in bank control	8	4	1	1	0	3
Charters	17	6	3	4	0	8
Conversions[c]	4	8	1	2	0	3
Federal branches	2	2	0	1	0	1
Fiduciary powers	13	9	2	0	0	2
Mergers[d]	71	70	43	8	0	51
Relocations	168	187	169	1	0	170
Reorganizations	49	71	52	12	0	64
Stock appraisals	0	0	0	0	0	0
Subsidiaries	58	107	24	0	0	24
12 CFR 5.53 change in assets	4	2	0	1	0	1
Limited national bank upgrade	0	1	0	0	0	0
Total	**1,475**	**1,608**	**1,340**	**40**	**0**	**1,382**

Source: OCC data.

[a] Data presented are for the fourth quarter of FY 2011 only.

[b] Total includes alternative decisions or no-objections.

[c] Conversions to national bank charters.

[d] Mergers include failure transactions when the national bank is the resulting institution.

Figure 2: Corporate Application Activity, Federal Savings Associations, FY 2011

	FY 2011	FY 2011 decisions				
	Applications received	Approved	Denied	Withdrawn	Transferred[a]	Total
Branches[b]	40	39	0	0	0	39
Bylaw/charter	8	7	0	1	0	8
Conditions	2	3	0	0	0	3
Control[c]	0	3	0	0	2	5
Conversions[d]	0	2	0	0	0	2
Holding company	3	5	0	0	5	10
Merger	1	4	0	0	0	4
New institution	0	0	0	0	0	0
Oakar	7	6	0	0	0	6
Operations[e]	31	36	1	8	2	47
Sasser	9	7	0	1	0	8
Subsidiaries	9	4	0	2	1	7
Waiver	3	2	0	1	31	34
Total	**113**	**118**	**1**	**13**	**41**	**173**

Source: National Applications Tracking System.

Note: Data presented are for the fourth quarter of FY 2011 only.

[a] Filings transferred to the Federal Reserve Board or FDIC under Dodd–Frank.

[b] Includes branch closings, change in location, interstate, and intrastate filings.

[c] Rebuttal of control filings.

[d] Mutual-to-stock conversions.

[e] Includes home office redesignation, director and senior officers, capital distribution, transfer of assets, voluntary dissolution, and golden parachute.

Figure 3: Licensing Actions and Timeliness, National Banks, FY 2010 and FY 2011

| | | FY 2010 | | | FY 2011 | | |
| | | | Within target | | | Within target | |
	Target time frames in days[a]	Number of decisions	Number	Percent	Number of decisions	Number	Percent
Branches	45/60	819	806	98	870	857	99
Capital/sub-debt	30/45	157	148	94	185	176	95
Change in bank control	NA/60	5	3	60	3	2	67
Charters[b]		12	8	67	8	7	88
Conversions	30/90	5	3	60	3	2	67
Federal branches	NA/120	0	0	0	1	1	100
Fiduciary powers	30/45	1	1	100	2	2	100
Mergers	45/60	64	61	95	51	49	96
Relocations	45/60	166	158	95	170	165	97
Reorganizations	45/60	45	40	89	64	58	91
Stock appraisals	NA/90	0	0	0	0	0	0
Subsidiaries	NA	65	61	94	24	21	88
12 CFR 5.53 change in assets	NA/60	5	5	100	1	1	100
Limited national bank upgrade		0	0	0	0	0	0
Total		**1,344**	**1,294**	**96**	**1,382**	**1,341**	**97**

Source: OCC data.

Note: Most decisions (95 percent in 2010 and 97 percent in 2011) were decided in he district offices and Large Bank Licensing under delegated authority. Decisions include approvals, conditional approvals, and denials. NA means not applicable.

[a] Those filings that qualified for the "expedited review" process are subject to the shorter time frames listed. The longer time frames are the standard benchmarks for more complex applications. New time frames commenced in 1997 with the adoption of the revised part 5. The target time frame may be extended if the OCC needs additional information to reach a decision, permits additional time for public comment, or processes a group of related filings as one transaction.

[b] For independent charter applications, the target time frame is 120 days. For holding-company-sponsored applications, the target time frame is 45 days for applications eligible for expedited review and 90 days for all others.

Figure 4: Change in Bank Control Act, National Banks, FY 2007–FY 2011
(Notices Processed With Disposition)

Year	Received	Acted on	Not disapproved	Disapproved	Withdrawn
2011	4	3	3	0	0
2010	8	5	5	0	0
2009	10	10	7	0	3
2008	5	4	4	0	0
2007	6	6	6	0	0

Source: OCC data.

Figure 5: Change in Bank Control Act, Federal Savings Associations, FY 2011
(Notices Processed With Disposition)[a]

Year	Received	Acted on	Not disapproved	Disapproved	Withdrawn
2011	0	3	3	0	0

Source: National Applications Tracking System.

[a] Data are for fourth quarter of FY 2011.

Figure 6: OCC Enforcement Actions, FY 2011

Type of enforcement action	Against institutions		Against institution-affiliated parties	
Cease-and-desist orders		43		11
Temporary cease-and-desist orders		0		0
12 USC 1818 civil money penalties		5		32
12 USC 1818 civil money penalties amount assessed	$	40,000,000	$	1,992,773
Flood insurance civil money penalties		3		0
Flood insurance civil money penalties amount assessed	$	3,895	$	0
Restitution orders		3		5
Amount of restitution ordered	$	54,268,745	$	4,541,970
Formal agreements		55		0
Capital directives		3		NA
Prompt corrective action directives		3		NA
Individual minimum capital ratio letters		50		NA
Safety and soundness orders		0		NA
Memorandums of understanding		16		0
Commitment letters		3		NA
Suspension orders		NA		1
12 USC 1818 removal/prohibition orders		NA		35
12 USC 1829 prohibitions		NA		133
Letters of reprimand		NA		23
Total		**184**		**240**

Note: NA means not applicable.

Figure 7: List of Applications Presenting Community Reinvestment Act Issues Decided, FY 2011

Bank, city, state	Interpretations and actions	Document number
First Niagara Bank, National Association, Buffalo, N.Y. (merger)	May 2011	CRA Decision No. 148
Harris National Association, Chicago, Illinois (conversion/merger)	July 2011	Corporate Decision No. 2011-10

Source: OCC data.

Future challenges will not deter the OCC from maintaining a strong internal control environment, or from pursuing a fiscally sound approach in operating the agency.

Section Six

Financial Management Discussion and Analysis

Letter From the Chief Financial Officer

I am pleased to present the OCC's financial statements as an integral part of the *Fiscal Year 2011 Annual Report*. For FY 2011, our independent auditors have again rendered an unqualified opinion with no material internal control weaknesses.

The financial statements include the assets and liabilities transferred to the OCC from the OTS on July 21, 2011, as required by Dodd–Frank, and they are presented in accordance with generally accepted accounting principles (GAAP) for U.S. federal agencies.

The foundation for an unqualified audit opinion begins with a strong internal control environment. For the past six years, the OCC has diligently applied the concepts and requirements embodied in the OMB's Circular A-123, "Management's Responsibility for Internal Control, Appendix A—Internal Control Over Financial Reporting." Once again, the OCC provided unqualified assurance that its internal control over financial reporting operated effectively and that no material weaknesses were found in the design or operation of those internal controls.

Annually, the Financial Management Department conducts a detailed risk assessment of the financial statements and applies rigorous tests of controls. This year's risk assessment includes the impact of assuming the bulk of the OTS's assets and liabilities. We performed a detailed analysis of the OTS balance sheet, and the results guided the proper classification of OTS accounts into the OCC's financial records.

While the impact of assuming the functions formerly performed by the OTS has been discussed throughout the *Annual Report,* I would like to take a few moments to review the financial impact of these changes. The OCC, which remains a nonappropriated agency after the passage of Dodd–Frank, continues to receive its main source of funding through assessments on national banks and, with the integration of the OTS, federal savings associations. These assessments are used to fund the OCC's operating costs, which include personnel, travel, and training. These three items alone represent 73 percent of the total annual operating budget.

Unused budgetary funds are placed into the OCC's financial reserves and are essential to the prudent financial management of the agency. These reserves allow

Thomas R. Bloom, Chief Financial Officer

the OCC to plan for structural changes to the national banking system, replace capital assets, and fund unanticipated, one-time needs—such as the impact of Dodd–Frank—without continuous changes to the bank assessment rate structure.

After careful analysis, the Financial Management Department determined that in FY 2012 the combined assessments from national banks and federal savings associations will be adequate to fund normal operations. Our analysis also shows that, overall, federal savings associations will pay less using the current OCC assessment structure. Although some federal savings associations will pay higher fees under the OCC assessment schedule, others will pay less. If all federal savings associations had been on the OCC assessment schedule in FY 2010, the federal savings association industry overall would have paid an estimated $18 million less in annual assessments.

This year, the OCC entered into a lease agreement for a new office building in Washington, D.C., to serve as the OCC's headquarters. The agreement enables the OCC to consolidate several office locations in Washington, provide the needed space to house former OTS staff, and realize the operating efficiencies afforded by such a move. In FY 2012, the OCC budget will include funding for leasehold improvements related to this new office space. It is anticipated that funds from the financial reserves will be used for this purpose.

In conjunction with the transfer of OTS assets and liabilities, the OCC assumed ownership of the OTS's former headquarters office building. While that property was not large enough to house the OCC headquarters, it is appropriate for the needs of the new CFPB. The OCC also assumed a significant pension liability, which it is required to fund according to

the provisions of Dodd–Frank. A discussion of this liability can be found in Note 8 to the Financial Statements. The OCC expects to be able to fund this liability through current operations and, if required, through the use of the agency's financial reserves.

While the OTS consolidation was a momentous priority, other structural changes occurred during the year to improve the overall operating efficiency of the OCC's administrative functions. The Information Technology Services (ITS) division was re-aligned to the Office of Management (OM). To improve the effectiveness and efficiency of the technology function, the ITS division was restructured and is adopting process improvement programs, such as Lean Six Sigma (LSS), currently in place in OM.

OM's LSS program was established in FY 2005 primarily to improve the processes at the OCC. Over time, this program has produced substantial cost savings and improved benchmark performance in many areas. In FY 2011, the OCC completed 16 business

process improvement projects, primarily with LSS, which resulted in $4.9 million of total cost savings. Since the inception of the program, 141 LSS projects have been completed with total cost savings or avoidance of $26.0 million. In addition, the OCC maintains a robust Black Belt and Green Belt training program. All OM executives have received formal training, and 46 staff members are certified as Master Black Belts, Black Belts, or Green Belts.

As we look forward to FY 2012 and beyond, the OCC will have the financial resources needed to accomplish its mission to supervise, charter, and regulate national banks and federal savings associations. While the coming year holds many challenges, it will not deter the OCC from maintaining a strong internal control environment, or from pursuing a fiscally sound approach in operating the agency.

Thomas R. Bloom
Chief Financial Officer

Financial Summary

The OCC received an unqualified opinion on its FY 2011 and FY 2010 financial statements. The OCC's financial statements consist of Balance Sheets, Statements of Net Cost, Statements of Changes in Net Position, and Statements of Budgetary Resources. The OCC presents the financial statements and notes on a comparative basis, providing financial information for FY 2011 and FY 2010. The financial statements were prepared from the OCC's accounting records in conformity with GAAP. The financial statements include the assets and liabilities that were transferred to the OCC from the OTS on July 21, 2011, the transfer date, as required by Dodd–Frank. The financial statements, followed by notes and the auditor's opinion, begin on page 52.

The following sections of the report address the OCC's financial activities in FY 2011 and FY 2010.

Office of Thrift Supervision Transfer

On July 21, 2010, President Obama signed Dodd–Frank into law. The act includes the Enhancing Financial Institution Safety and Soundness Act of 2010, which transferred all of the OTS's assets and liabilities to the OCC on July 21, 2011, at book value as of the close of business on July 20, 2011. The transfer of the OTS balance sheet complies with GAAP.

The fluctuations caused by the transfer-in of assets and liabilities from the OTS are discussed in more detail below.

Assets totaling $321.0 million and liabilities totaling in excess of $50.1 million were transferred to the OCC's Balance Sheet. The majority of the transfer of net assets includes $284.6 million in the fund balance with Treasury (FBWT) and $24.7 million from the land and a building owned by the OTS. Actuarial liabilities of $24.7 million, including the Pentegra Defined Benefit Plan for Financial Institutions (Pentegra DB Plan), formerly known as the Financial Institutions Retirement Fund, annual leave of $13.0 million, and $10.4 million in payroll-related liabilities, represent the majority of the transfer of liabilities.

Under the provisions of Dodd–Frank, in FY 2011 the OCC assumed the cost of the Pentegra DB Plan, a special retirement system in which some of the transferred OTS employees participate. The current fund target for this significant pension liability is $481.3 million, with plan assets of $406.5 million and an estimated minimum required contribution to the FY 2012 plan year of $36.1 million. The OCC expects to be able to fund the costs associated with this liability using assets transferred from the OTS. The remaining costs will be funded as required through current operations.

The figure below shows the full impact of the OTS transfer of assets and liabilities to the OCC.

OTS Transfer (in Millions)

	FY 2011
Fund balance with Treasury	$ 284.6
Accounts receivable	9.6
Building and land	24.7
Equipment and leasehold improvements	2.1
Total assets (net)	**$ 321.0**
Accrued liabilities	2.0
Accrued payroll and benefits	10.4
Accrued annual leave	13.0
Accrued postretirement benefits	24.7
Total liabilities	**$ 50.1**
Net position	270.9
Total liabilities and net position	**$ 321.0**

Source: OCC financial system data.

Assets

The OCC's assets include both "entity" and "non-entity" assets. The OCC uses entity assets, which belong to the agency, to fund operations. The OCC acquires revenue through the collection of assessments from national banks and federal savings associations and from other income, including interest on investments in U.S. Treasury securities. Non-entity assets are assets that the OCC holds on behalf of another federal agency. The OCC's non-entity assets presented as accounts receivable are civil money penalties due the federal government through court-enforced legal actions.

As of September 30, 2011, total assets were $1,526.6 million, an increase of $414.8 million, or 37.3 percent, from the level on September 30, 2010. The majority of this increase is attributable to the transfer of assets, including those from the liquidation of the OTS's long-term investments prior to the transfer date as reflected in the FBWT and other assets amount shown in the figure below. Also included were fixed assets, notably the land and a building owned by the OTS. The remaining increase is primarily attributable to the growth in the OCC's investment portfolio. Investments and related interest rose by $143.5 million, or 13.7 percent, due in part to the transfer of assets, which resulted in an increase in operating cash and, subsequently, the ability to invest additional funds in overnight securities.

Figure 8 shows the OCC's composition of assets for FY 2011 and FY 2010.

Figure 8: Composition of Assets (in Millions)

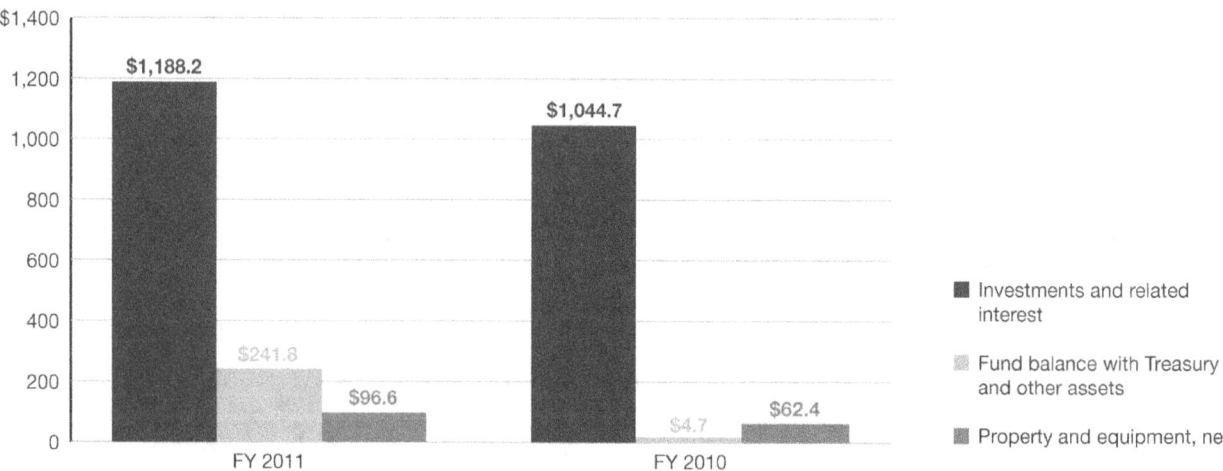

Source: OCC financial system data.

Liabilities

The OCC's liabilities represent the resources due to others or held for future recognition and are composed largely of deferred revenue, accrued liabilities, and accounts payable. Deferred revenue represents the unearned portion of semiannual assessments that have been collected but not earned.

As of September 30, 2011, total liabilities were $430.8 million, a net increase of $104.4 million, or 32.0 percent, over the level on September 30, 2010. The increase of $41.1 million, or 21.1 percent, in deferred revenue was a result of an increase in assessment collections during FY 2011, the majority of which is attributable to assessments collected from federal savings associations that the OCC now supervises. The majority of the increase of $27.3 million, or 25.8 percent, in accounts payable and accrued liabilities was caused by an increase in payroll and employee benefits, primarily a result of the transfer of 670 former OTS employees to the OCC on July 21, 2011.

Figure 9 illustrates the OCC's composition of liabilities for FY 2011 and FY 2010.

Figure 9: Composition of Liabilities (in Millions)

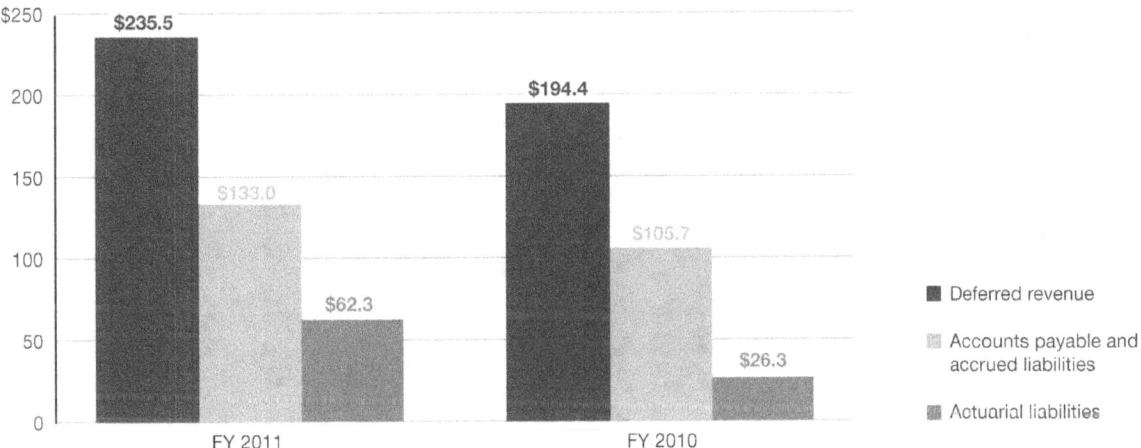

Source: OCC financial system data.

Net Position

The OCC's net position of $1,095.8 million as of September 30, 2011, and $785.5 million as of September 30, 2010, represent the cumulative net excess of the OCC's revenues over the cost of operations since inception and includes the transfer-in of $270.9 million from the OTS. The majority of the increase of $310.3 million, or 39.5 percent, is directly attributable to the transfer of the OTS net position. The net position is presented on both the Balance Sheets and the Statements of Changes in Net Position.

The OCC reserves a significant portion of the net position to supplement resources made available to fund the OCC's annual budget and to cover foreseeable but rare events or new requirements and opportunities. The OCC also sets aside funds for ongoing operations to cover undelivered orders, the consumption of assets, and capital investments.

Figure 10 shows the OCC's composition of net position for FY 2011 and FY 2010.

Figure 10: Composition of Net Position (in Millions)

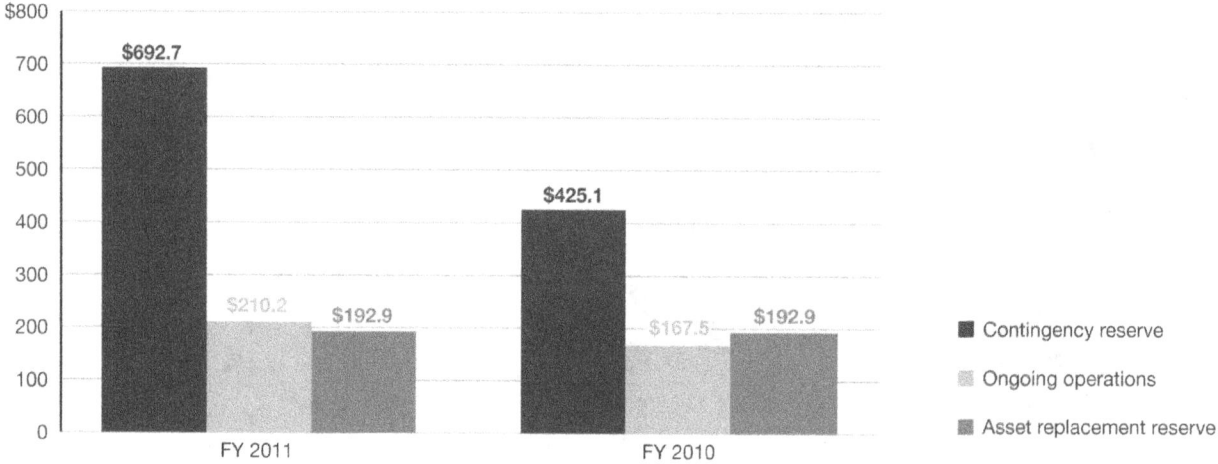

Source: OCC financial system data.

Reserves

The establishment of financial reserves is integral to the effective stewardship of the OCC's resources, particularly because the agency does not receive congressional appropriations. The contingency reserve reduces the impact on the OCC's operations from revenue shortfalls, from unanticipated expenses resulting from foreseeable but rare events that are beyond the OCC's control, or from new requirements and opportunities. Examples of such events might include a major change in the national banking system, a fire or flood, or significant impairment to the OCC's information technology network that interferes with the OCC's ability to accomplish its mission.

These reserves also allow the OCC to fund special one-time needs, such as those that arose from the regulatory restructuring required by Dodd–Frank, and which could include the funding of the Pentegra DB Plan liability transferred from the OTS. In FY 2011, the transfer of the OTS's net position caused the significant increase in the contingency reserve. The asset replacement reserve is for the replacement of information technology investments, leasehold improvements, and furniture replacement for future years. During FY 2011, the OCC entered into a long-term lease for a new headquarters office building for which the leasehold improvements will be funded from the asset replacement reserve.

Revenues and Costs

The OCC's operations are funded primarily by assessments collected from national banks and federal savings associations and from interest received on investments in U.S. Treasury securities. The OCC, in accordance with 12 USC 482, establishes budget authority for a given fiscal year. The total budget authority available for use by the OCC in FY 2011 was $876.5 million, which represents an increase of $84.8 million, or 10.7 percent, over the $791.7 million budget in FY 2010 and includes $62.0 million in budget authority transferred from the OTS.

Total FY 2011 revenue of $843.2 million reflects a $56.5 million, or 7.2 percent, increase over FY 2010 revenues of $786.7 million. The increase is largely attributable to asset growth in the national banking system and the collection of assessments from the federal savings associations that the OCC began supervising in FY 2011. Total national bank assets under OCC supervision rose as of June 30, 2011, to $8.8 trillion, up 3.5 percent from $8.5 trillion a year earlier. Of this total, $7.7 trillion, or 87.5 percent, is attributable to large national banks. Midsize and community banks' share represents $915.1 billion, or 10.2 percent, followed by federal branches at $179.4 billion, or 2.3 percent. Although not yet consolidated with the OCC, the OTS had thrift assets totaling $908.3 billion as of June 30, 2011.

Figure 11 depicts the components of total revenue for FY 2011 and FY 2010.

Figure 11: Components of Total Revenue (in Millions)

	FY 2011	FY 2010	Change ($)	Change (%)
Assessments	$ 814.6	$ 764.4	$ 50.2	6.6%
Investments and other income[a]	28.6	22.3	6.3	28.3
Total revenue	$ 843.2	$ 786.7	$ 56.5	7.2%

Source: OCC financial system data.

[a] Other sources of revenue include reimbursable activities and other miscellaneous sources.

Investments

The book value of the OCC's investment portfolio on September 30, 2011, was $1,184.6 million, compared with $1,041.1 million a year earlier. The market value of the OCC's portfolio in excess of book value rose to $38.9 million from $37.9 million on September 30, 2010. The OCC invests available funds in non-marketable U.S. Treasury securities issued through the Treasury Department's Bureau of Public Debt in accordance with the provisions of 12 USC 481 and 12 USC 192. The OCC manages risk by diversifying its portfolio across maturities within established parameters. Diversifying maturities of the individual securities is meant to help manage the inherent risk of interest-rate fluctuations. The weighted average maturity of the OCC's investment portfolio as of September 30, 2011, and September 30, 2010, was 1.62 years and 1.87 years, respectively. The portfolio earned an annual yield for FY 2011 of 2.3 percent, compared with 2.6 percent in FY 2010. The OCC calculates annual portfolio yield by dividing the total interest earned during the year by the average ending monthly book value of investments.

Cost of Operations

The OCC's net cost of operations is reported on the Statements of Net Cost and the Statements of Changes in Net Position. The OCC uses an activity-based time reporting system to allocate costs among the agency's programs. Costs are further divided into those resulting from transactions between the OCC and other federal entities (intragovernmental) and those between the OCC and nonfederal entities (with the public). The Statements of Net Cost present the full cost of operating the OCC's three major programs—supervise, regulate, and charter national banks. FY 2011 data include the costs associated with operating these programs beginning July 21, 2011, for federal savings associations.

Figure 12 illustrates the breakdown of costs of operations by major program for FY 2011 and FY 2010.

Figure 12: Costs of Operations by Major Program (in Millions)

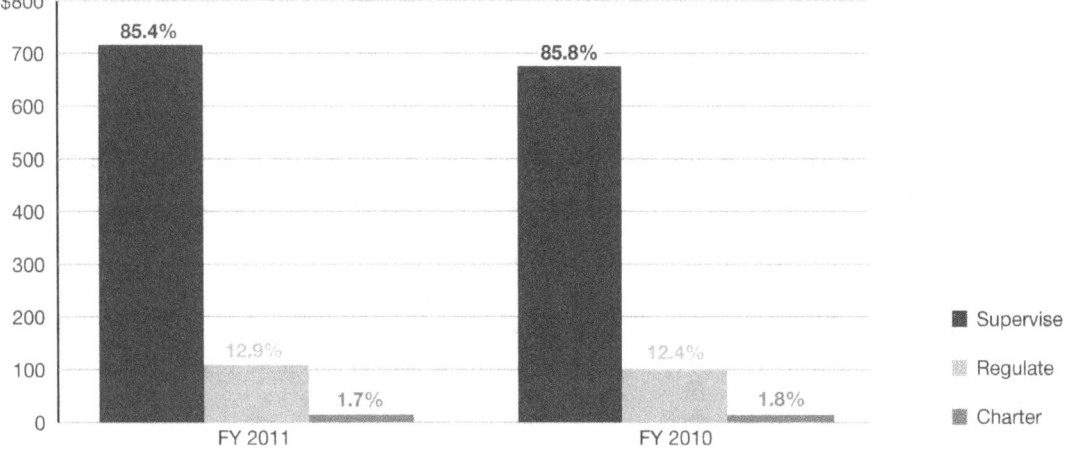

Source: OCC financial system data.

The full cost presented in the Statements of Net Cost includes costs contributed by the Office of Personnel Management (OPM) on behalf of the OCC to cover the cost of the Federal Employees Retirement System (FERS) and Civil Service Retirement System (CSRS) retirement plans and the Federal Employees Health Benefits (FEHB) and Federal Employees' Group Life Insurance (FEGLI) plans, totaling $33.7 million in FY 2011 and $32.9 million in FY 2010. FY 2011 total program costs of $837.7 million reflect an increase of $51.1 million, or 6.5 percent, from $786.6 million in FY 2010. The increase was primarily due to an increase in the cost of pay and benefits, including those for former OTS employees who were transferred to the OCC. Additional contributing factors include increases to contractual services for systems maintenance, rent, and travel costs.

The full cost is reduced by earned revenues to arrive at net cost. Earned revenues increased by $56.5 million, or 7.2 percent, to $843.2 million in FY 2011, due to an increase in FY 2011 bank assessments that was slightly offset by minor decreases in other revenues. The increases in assessments are a direct result of bank asset growth in both the national banking system, particularly the largest banks, and the federal savings association industry.

Correspondingly, the costs of supervising the national banks and federal savings associations have risen because of the increasing size and complexity of their assets.

Budgetary Resources

The Statements of Budgetary Resources, found on page 55, provide information about how budgetary resources were made available to the OCC for the year and present the status of these resources and the net outlay of budgetary resources at the end of the year. The OCC executed $819.5 million, or 93.5 percent, of the FY 2011 budget of $876.5 million.

Office of the Comptroller of the Currency
Balance Sheets

As of September 30, 2011 and 2010

(in Thousands)

	2011	2010
Assets		
Intragovernmental:		
Fund balance with Treasury (Note 2)	$ 237,036	$ 3,981
Investments and related interest (Note 3)	1,188,159	1,044,678
Accounts receivable (Note 4)	3,931	0
Other assets	316	0
Total intragovernmental	**1,429,442**	**1,048,659**
Accounts receivable, net (Note 4)	542	661
Property and equipment, net (Note 5)	96,617	62,460
Other assets	24	49
Total assets	**$ 1,526,625**	**$ 1,111,829**
Liabilities		
Intragovernmental:		
Accounts payable and other accrued liabilities	$ 3,300	$ 2,489
Total intragovernmental	**3,300**	**2,489**
Accounts payable	8,056	9,772
Accrued payroll and benefits	43,811	32,463
Accrued annual leave	47,630	37,476
Other accrued liabilities	30,249	23,442
Deferred revenue	235,514	194,443
Other actuarial liabilities (Note 8)	62,272	26,290
Total liabilities	**430,832**	**326,375**
Net position (Note 9)	**1,095,793**	**785,454**
Total liabilities and net position	**$ 1,526,625**	**$ 1,111,829**

The accompanying notes are an integral part of these financial statements.

Office of the Comptroller of the Currency

Statements of Net Cost

For the Years Ended September 30, 2011 and 2010

(in Thousands)

	2011		2010	
Program costs				
Supervise				
Intragovernmental	$	103,977	$	94,707
With the public		611,387		580,615
Subtotal—supervise	$	715,364	$	675,322
Regulate				
Intragovernmental	$	16,003	$	13,972
With the public		91,977		83,415
Subtotal—regulate	$	107,980	$	97,387
Charter				
Intragovernmental	$	2,212	$	2,063
With the public		12,148		11,796
Subtotal—charter	$	14,360	$	13,859
Total program costs	$	837,704	$	786,568
Less: earned revenues not attributed to programs		(843,203)		(786,717)
Net program costs before gain/loss from				
changes in assumptions	$	(5,499)	$	(149)
Actuarial (gain)/loss (Note 8)		(196)		1,903
Net cost of operations (Note 10)	$	(5,695)	$	1,754

The accompanying notes are an integral part of these financial statements.

Office of the Comptroller of the Currency
Statements of Changes in Net Position
For the Years Ended September 30, 2011 and 2010
(in Thousands)

	2011	2010
Beginning balances	$ 785,454	$ 754,318
Budgetary financing sources:		
Transfer-in without reimbursement (Note 13)	259,222	0
Other financing sources:		
Transfer-in without reimbursement (Note 13)	11,675	0
Imputed financing (Note 11)	33,747	32,890
Net cost of operations	5,695	(1,754)
Net change	310,339	31,136
Ending balances	$ **1,095,793**	$ **785,454**

The accompanying notes are an integral part of these financial statements.

Office of the Comptroller of the Currency
Statements of Budgetary Resources
For the Years Ended September 30, 2011 and 2010

(in Thousands)

		2011		2010
Budgetary resources				
Unobligated balance, brought forward, October 1	$	847,259	$	793,371
Spending authority from offsetting collections				
Earned				
Collected		891,591		794,029
Receivable from federal sources		3,914		79
Subtotal		895,505		794,108
Nonexpenditure transfer, net, actual		245,034		0
Total budgetary resources	$	**1,987,798**	$	**1,587,479**
Status of budgetary resources				
Obligations incurred	$	824,994	$	740,220
Unobligated balance available		1,162,804		847,259
Total status of budgetary resources	$	**1,987,798**	$	**1,587,479**
Change in obligated balance				
Obligated balance, net, beginning of period				
Unpaid obligations brought forward, October 1	$	184,501	$	177,517
Uncollected customer payments from federal sources, October 1		(3,579)		(3,500)
Total unpaid obligated balance, net		180,922		174,017
Obligations incurred		824,994		740,220
Gross outlays		(797,892)		(733,236)
Obligated balance transfer, net				
Unpaid obligations transferred		39,562		0
Uncollected customer payments from federal sources transferred		0		0
Total unpaid obligated balance transferred, net		39,562		0
Change in uncollected customer payments from federal sources		(3,914)		(79)
Obligated balance, net, end of period				
Unpaid obligations		251,164		184,501
Uncollected customer payments from federal sources		(7,493)		(3,579)
Obligated balance, net, end of period		243,671		180,922
Net outlays				
Gross outlays	$	797,892	$	733,236
Offsetting collections		(891,591)		(794,029)
Net outlays	$	**(93,699)**	$	**(60,793)**

The accompanying notes are an integral part of these financial statements.

Notes to the Financial Statements

Note 1—Significant Accounting Policies

A. Reporting Entity

The OCC was created as a bureau within the Treasury Department by an act of Congress in 1863. The mission of the OCC was to establish and regulate a system of federally chartered national banks. The National Currency Act of 1863, rewritten and reenacted as the National Bank Act of 1864, authorized the OCC to supervise national banks and to regulate the lending and investment activities of federally chartered institutions. With the passage of Dodd–Frank on July 21, 2010, the OCC now also oversees federally chartered savings associations.

The financial statements report on the OCC's three major programs: supervise, regulate, and charter national banks and federal savings associations. The OCC's major programs support the agency's overall mission by ensuring a safe and sound system of national banks and federal savings associations (collectively, banks); promoting equal access to financial services and fair treatment of bank customers; maintaining a flexible legal and regulatory framework that enables a strong, competitive system of banks; and having a competent, highly motivated, and diverse workforce.

B. Basis of Accounting and Presentation

The accompanying financial statements present the operations of the OCC, which include the recently transferred OTS functions. The OCC's financial statements are prepared from the agency's accounting records in conformity with GAAP as set forth by the Federal Accounting Standards Advisory Board (FASAB). The OCC's financial statements are presented in accordance with the form and content guidelines established by the OMB in Circular No. A-136, "Financial Reporting Requirements."

In addition, the OCC applies financial accounting and reporting standards issued by the Financial Accounting Standards Board only as outlined in Statement of Federal Financial Accounting Standards (SFFAS) 34, "The Hierarchy of Generally Accepted Accounting Principles," including the "Application of Standards Issued by the Financial Accounting Standards Board."

The OCC's financial statements consist of Balance Sheets, Statements of Net Cost, Statements of Changes in Net Position, and Statements of Budgetary Resources. The OCC presents its financial statements on a comparative basis, providing information for FY 2011 and FY 2010. Fiscal year 2011 data include balances transferred from the OTS financial statements for the period ending July 20, 2011, and activity of the combined entity from the transfer date through September 30, 2011. The FY 2010 financial statements represent OCC financial information as originally published, before the consolidation.

The financial statements reflect both the accrual and budgetary bases of accounting. Under the accrual basis of accounting, revenues are recognized when earned, and expenses are recognized when a liability is incurred, without regard to cash receipt or payment. The budgetary method recognizes the obligation of funds according to legal requirements, which in many cases is recorded before the occurrence of an accrual-based transaction. Budgetary accounting is essential for compliance with legal constraints and controls over the use of federal funds.

In accordance with GAAP, the preparation of financial statements requires management to make estimates and assumptions that affect the reported amounts of assets and liabilities, the disclosure of contingent assets and liabilities at the date of the financial statements, and the reported amounts of revenue and expense during the reporting period. Such estimates and assumptions could change in the future as more information becomes known, which could affect the amounts reported and disclosed herein.

Throughout these financial statements, assets, liabilities, earned revenues, and costs have been classified according to the entity responsible for these transactions. Intragovernmental earned revenues are collections or accruals of revenue from other federal entities, and intragovernmental costs are payments or accruals of expenditures to other federal entities.

C. Revenues and Other Financing Sources

The OCC derives its revenue primarily from assessments and fees paid by national banks and federal savings associations, and from income on investments in nonmarketable U.S. Treasury securities. The OCC does not receive congressional appropriations to fund any of the agency's operations. Therefore, the OCC has no unexpended appropriations.

By federal statute 12 USC 481, the OCC's funds are maintained in both a U.S. government trust revolving fund and a non-trust revolving fund. The funds remain available to cover the annual costs of the OCC's operations in accordance with policies established by the Comptroller of the Currency.

D. Earmarked Funds

Earmarked funds are financed by specifically identified revenues, often supplemented by other financing sources, which remain available over time. These specifically identified revenues and other financing sources are required by statute to be used for designated activities, benefits, or purposes, and must be accounted for separately from the government's general revenues. In accordance with FASAB SFFAS No. 27, "Identifying and Reporting Earmarked Funds," all of the OCC's revenue meets this criterion and constitutes an earmarked fund.

E. Fund Balance With Treasury

The Treasury Department processes the OCC's cash receipts and disbursements. Sufficient funds are maintained in two U.S. government revolving funds and are available to pay current liabilities. The OCC's Statements of Budgetary Resources reflect the status of the agency's FBWT.

F. Investments

It is the OCC's policy to invest available funds in accordance with the provisions of 12 USC 481 and 12 USC 192. The OCC invests available funds in non-marketable

U.S. Treasury securities, which may include one-day certificates, bills, notes, and bonds. The OCC does not invest funds with state or national banks. The OCC has the positive intent and ability to hold all U.S. Treasury securities to maturity in accordance with Statement of Financial Accounting Standard (SFAS) No. 115, "Accounting for Certain Investments in Debt and Equity Securities," and does not maintain any available-for-sale or trading securities.

G. Accounts Receivable

In accordance with SFFAS No. 1, "Accounting for Selected Assets and Liabilities," the OCC updates the "allowance for loss on accounts receivable" account annually or as needed to reflect the most current estimate of accounts that are likely to be uncollectible. Accounts receivable from the public are reduced by an allowance for loss on doubtful accounts.

H. Property and Equipment

Property and equipment as well as internal-use software are accounted for in accordance with SFFAS No. 6, "Accounting for Property, Plant, and Equipment," and SFFAS No. 10, "Accounting for Internal Use Software."

Property and equipment purchases and additions are stated at cost. The OCC expenses acquisitions that do not meet the capitalization criteria, such as normal repairs and maintenance, when they are received or incurred.

In addition, property and equipment are depreciated or amortized, as applicable, over their estimated useful lives using the straight-line

method. They are removed from the OCC's asset accounts in the period of disposal, retirement, or removal from service. Any difference between the book value of the property and equipment and amounts realized is recognized as a gain or loss in the same period that the asset is removed.

I. Liabilities

The OCC records liabilities for amounts that are likely to be paid as a result of events that have occurred as of the relevant Balance Sheet dates. The OCC's liabilities consist of routine operating accounts payable, accrued payroll and benefits, and deferred revenue. The OCC's liabilities represent the amounts owed or accrued under contractual or other arrangements governing the transactions, including operating expenses incurred but not paid. The OCC accounts for liabilities in accordance with SFFAS No. 5, "Accounting for Liabilities of the Federal Government."

Accounts Payable

Payments are made in a timely manner in accordance with the Prompt Payment Act. Interest penalties are paid when payments are late. Discounts are taken when cost effective and when the invoice is paid within the discount period.

Accrued Annual Leave

In accordance with SFFAS No. 5, annual leave is accrued and funded by the OCC as it is earned, and the accrual is reduced as leave is taken or paid. Each year, the balance in the accrued annual leave account is adjusted to reflect actual leave balances with current pay rates. Sick leave and other types of leave are expensed as incurred.

Deferred Revenue

The OCC's activities are primarily financed by assessments on assets held by national banks, federal savings associations, and the federal branches of foreign banks. These assessments are due March 31 and September 30 of each year, based on their asset balances as of December 31 and June 30, respectively. Assessments are paid mid-cycle and are recognized as earned revenue on a straight-line basis. The unearned portions of collected assessments are classified as deferred revenue.

J. Employment Benefits

Retirement Plans

All of the OCC's employees participate in one of three retirement systems—two administered by OPM (CSRS and FERS) and one for which the OCC assumed the role of benefit administrator in FY 2011 (the Pentegra DB Plan). Pursuant to the enactment of Public Law 99-335, which established FERS, most OCC employees hired after December 31, 1983, are automatically covered by FERS and Social Security. Employees hired before January 1, 1984, are covered by CSRS, with the exception of those who, during the election period, joined FERS.

The OCC does not report CSRS or FERS assets or accumulated plan benefits that may be applicable to its employees in its financial statements; OPM reports them. Although the OCC reports no liability for future payments to employees under these programs, the federal government is liable for future payments to employees through the various agencies administering these programs.

As benefit administrator for the Pentegra DB Plan—in which some of the transferred OTS employees participate and which is closed to new entrants—the OCC is committed to adhering to sound financial policies and management oversight of the plan to ensure its sustainability for current and future retirees.

Thrift Savings Plan

The OCC's employees are eligible to participate in the federal Thrift Savings Plan. For employees under FERS, a Thrift Savings Plan account is automatically established, and the OCC contributes a mandatory 1.0 percent of base pay to this account. The OCC also matches employee contributions up to an additional 4.0 percent of pay, for a maximum OCC contribution of 5.0 percent of base pay.

OCC 401(k) Plans

In addition to the federal Thrift Savings Plan, OCC employees can elect to contribute a portion of their base pay to the OCC-sponsored 401(k) plan, subject to Internal Revenue Service regulations that apply to employee contributions in both the federal Thrift Savings Plan and the OCC-sponsored 401(k) plan.

As required by law, for OTS employees transferred to the OCC, the OCC continues to offer a separate 401(k) plan. The amount of each participant's matching contribution is based on the applicable retirement system under which each participant is covered.

Federal Employees Health Benefits and Federal Employees' Group Life Insurance

Employees and retirees of the OCC are eligible to participate in the FEHB and FEGLI plans administered by OPM that involve a cost sharing of biweekly coverage premiums by employee and employer. The OCC does not fund post-retirement benefits for these programs. Instead, the OCC's financial statements recognize an imputed financing source and corresponding expense that represent the OCC's share of the cost to the federal government of providing these benefits to all eligible OCC employees.

Post-retirement Life Insurance Benefit Plan

The OCC sponsors a life insurance benefit plan for current and retired employees. This plan is a defined benefit plan for which the benefit is earned over the period from the employee's date of hire to the date on which the employee is assumed to retire. The valuation of the plan is conducted in accordance with generally accepted actuarial principles and practices, including the applicable Actuarial Standards of Practice as issued by the Actuarial Standards Board. Specifically, the OCC uses the actuarial cost method as outlined in SFAS No. 87, "Employers' Accounting for Pensions," to determine costs for its retirement plans. Gains or losses owing to changes in actuarial assumptions are amortized over the service life of the plan. The actuarial assumptions and methods used in calculating actuarial amounts comply with the requirements for post-retirement benefits other than pensions as set forth in SFAS No. 106, "Employers' Accounting for Postretirement Benefits Other Than Pensions," and for health benefit plans as set forth in American Institute of Certified Public Accountants Statement of Position 92-6.

In addition, for the one-year period following the transfer date, the OCC will continue to administer a separate life insurance plan for those OTS employees transferred to the OCC who meet eligibility requirements.

K. Custodial Revenues and Collections

Non-entity receivables, liabilities, and revenue are recorded as custodial activity and include amounts collected for fines, civil money penalties, and related interest assessments. Revenues are recognized as cash collected that will be transferred to the General Fund of the U.S. Treasury at the end of the fiscal year.

L. Effects of Recent Accounting Pronouncements

In FY 2010, the OCC began displaying gains and losses from changes in long-term assumptions

used to estimate federal employee pensions, other retirement benefits, and other post-employment benefit liabilities as a separate line item on the Statements of Net Cost in accordance with the guidance outlined in SFFAS No. 33, "Pensions, Other Retirement Benefits, and Other Postemployment Benefits: Reporting the Gains and Losses From Changes in Assumptions and Selecting Discount Rates and Valuation Dates."

On August 4, 2010, the FASAB published SFFAS No. 39, "Subsequent Events: Codification of Accounting and Financial Reporting Standards Contained in the AICPA [American Institute of Certified Public Accountants] Statements on Auditing Standards." This statement does not establish new accounting guidance but rather incorporates the existing guidance (to the extent appropriate in the federal government environment) into the FASAB standards. The statement's requirements improve financial reporting by incorporating authoritative accounting and financial reporting literature into a single source and thereby better enabling entities to prepare basic information and required supplementary information in conformity with GAAP. The statement addresses the circumstances under which an entity should recognize or disclose events or transactions occurring after the end of the reporting period but before issuance of the financial report. The OCC adopted SFFAS No. 39 upon issuance, as required, without material effect.

Note 2—Fund Balance With Treasury

The status of the FBWT represents the budgetary resources that support the FBWT and is a reconciliation between budgetary and proprietary accounts. The OCC's FBWT comprises two separate U.S. Treasury fund symbols. The first is designated as a trust fund established by 12 USC 481 that governs the collection and use of assessments and other funds by the OCC. The second is a new fund symbol designated as a revolving fund and was established to allow for the transfer of OTS funds to the OCC on July 21, 2011. The OCC's FBWT consists of unobligated and obligated balances that reflect the budgetary authority remaining for disbursement against current or future obligations.

The unobligated balance represents the cumulative amount of budgetary authority that has not been set aside to cover outstanding obligations and is classified as available for future OCC use without further congressional action. The obligated balance not yet disbursed represents funds that have been obligated for goods that have not been received or services that have not been performed. It also represents goods and services that have been delivered or received but for which payment has not been made. The nonbudgetary FBWT account represents adjustments to budgetary accounts that do not affect the FBWT. The OCC's balance represents investment accounts that reduce the status of the FBWT.

The figure below depicts the OCC's FBWT amounts for FY 2011 and FY 2010.

Fund Balance With Treasury (in Thousands)

	FY 2011		FY 2010	
Fund balance:				
Revolving fund	$	226,413	$	0
Trust fund		10,623		3,981
Total fund balance	$	237,036	$	3,981
Status of fund balance with Treasury				
Unobligated balance—available	$	1,162,804	$	847,259
Obligated balance not yet disbursed		243,671		180,922
Non-budgetary fund balance with Treasury		(1,169,439)		(1,024,200)
Total	$	237,036	$	3,981

Note 3—Investments and Related Interest

The OCC's investments are stated at amortized cost and the related accrued interest. Premiums and discounts are amortized over the term of the investment using the effective interest method.

The fair market value of investment securities was $1,223.5 million on September 30, 2011, and $1,079.0 million on September 30, 2010. The overall portfolio earned an annual yield of 2.3 percent for FY 2011 and 2.6 percent for FY 2010.

The yield-to-maturity on the non-overnight portion of the OCC's investment portfolio ranged from 0.9 percent to 4.5 percent in FY 2011 and from 0.7 percent to 4.5 percent in FY 2010.

FY 2011 Investments and Related Interest (in Thousands)

	Cost	Amortization method	Amortized (premium) discount	Investments, net	Market value disclosure
Intragovernmental securities:					
Non-marketable market-based	$ 1,192,820	Effective interest	$ (8,224)	$ 1,184,596	$ 1,223,491
Accrued interest	3,563		0	3,563	3,563
Total intragovernmental investments	$ 1,196,383		$ (8,224)	$ 1,188,159	$ 1,227,054

FY 2010 Investments and Related Interest (in Thousands)

	Cost	Amortization method	Amortized (premium) discount	Investments, net	Market value disclosure
Intragovernmental securities:					
Non-marketable market-based	$ 1,048,359	Effective interest	$ (7,260)	$ 1,041,099	$ 1,079,001
Accrued interest	3,579		0	3,579	3,579
Total intragovernmental investments	$ 1,051,938		$ (7,260)	$ 1,044,678	$ 1,082,580

Note 4—Accounts Receivable

As presented in the OCC's Balance Sheets, accounts receivable represent monies due from the public, for services and goods provided that are retained by the OCC upon collection. The amounts shown for federal receivables represent pension sharing costs for OTS employees transferred to other federal agencies rather than to the OCC. Also included are civil money penalty (CMP) amounts assessed against people, national banks, or federal savings associations for violations of law, regulation, and orders; unsafe or unsound practices; and breaches of fiduciary duty. Because CMPs are not debts due the OCC, the amount outstanding does not enter into the calculation for the allowance for uncollectible accounts. The OCC has recognized $41.6 million and $50.7 million in CMP non-entity revenue as of September 30, 2011 and 2010, respectively.

FY 2011 Accounts Receivable (in Thousands)

	Gross	Allowance for uncollectible accounts	Accounts receivable, net
Federal receivables	$ 3,931	$ 0	$ 3,931
Civil money penalties receivables	486	0	486
Nonfederal receivables	81	(25)	56
Total accounts receivable	**$ 4,498**	**$ (25)**	**$ 4,473**

FY 2010 Accounts Receivable (in Thousands)

	Gross	Allowance for uncollectible accounts	Accounts receivable, net
Civil money penalties receivables	$ 643	$ 0	$ 643
Nonfederal receivables	45	(27)	18
Total accounts receivable	**$ 688**	**$ (27)**	**$ 661**

Note 5—Property and Equipment, Net

Property and equipment purchased at a cost greater than or equal to the noted thresholds below with useful lives of three years or more are capitalized at cost and depreciated or amortized, as applicable. Depreciation is expensed on a straight-line basis over the estimated useful life of the asset with the exception of leasehold improvements. Leasehold improvements are amortized on a straight-line basis over the lesser of the terms of the related leases or their estimated useful lives.

Land, leasehold improvements in development, and internal-use software in development are not depreciated. Major alterations and renovations, including leasehold and land improvements, are capitalized, while maintenance and repair costs are charged to expenses as incurred. All other property and equipment are depreciated or amortized, as applicable, on a straight-line basis over their estimated useful lives.

For FY 2011 and FY 2010, the OCC reported $1.9 million and $312.3 thousand, respectively, of

fully depreciated assets removed from service. In FY 2011, there was no gain or loss on asset disposal. In FY 2010, the OCC recognized a loss of $5.7 million on the disposal of other assets. The figures below summarize property and equipment balances as of September 30, 2011 and 2010.

FY 2011 assets include the land and a building owned by the OTS that were transferred to the OCC on July 21, 2011. The building is a rental income property that the OCC uses to supplement its operating budget. See Note 6.

FY 2011 Property and Equipment, Net (in Thousands)

Class of assets	Capitalization threshold	Useful life	Cost	Accumulated depreciation/ amortization	Net book value
Land	NA	NA	$ 7,101	$ 0	$ 7,101
Building	50	50	49,188	(31,812)	17,376
Leasehold improvements	50	5–20	78,766	(48,536)	30,230
Equipment	50	3–10	30,918	(24,170)	6,748
Internal use software	500	5	69,025	(57,797)	11,228
Internal use software—development	500	NA	19,990	0	19,990
Leasehold improvements—development	50	NA	3,944	0	3,944
Total			**$ 258,932**	**$ (162,315)**	**$ 96,617**

FY 2010 Property and Equipment, Net (in Thousands)

Class of assets	Capitalization threshold	Useful life	Cost	Accumulated depreciation/ amortization	Net book value
Land	NA	NA	$ 0	$ 0	$ 0
Building	50	50	0	0	0
Leasehold improvements	50	5–20	71,974	(37,701)	34,273
Equipment	50	3–10	27,180	(21,662)	5,518
Internal use software	500	5	63,496	(51,948)	11,548
Internal use software—development	500	NA	9,858	0	9,858
Leasehold improvements—development	50	NA	1,263	0	1,263
Total			**$ 173,771**	**$ (111,311)**	**$ 62,460**

Note: NA means not applicable.

Note 6—Rental Income

Before the transfer date, the OTS leased a portion of its former headquarters building as office and retail space under non-cancellable operating leases expiring at various dates through 2021. Some of these leases provide renewal options. The leases provide for annual base rent and additional rents for building operating expenses. Some leases provide for fixed future increases in rents over the term of the lease. After the transfer date, the OCC assumed ownership over the leases and received rental income from both existing and new tenants.

The future minimum rentals to be received under non-cancellable operating lease arrangements, not including renewals, are shown below.

The OCC has been negotiating an occupancy agreement with another federal agency for the remaining space at the OTS's former headquarters. The figure below does not include anticipated future rental income for the OCC.

FY 2011 Future Rental Income (in Thousands)

Year	Amount
2012	$ 2,468
2013	647
2014	599
2015	374
2016	305
2017 and beyond	1,141
Total	$ 5,534

Note 7—Leases

The OCC leases equipment and office space for its Headquarters operations in Washington, D.C., and for district and field operations. During FY 2011, the OTS transferred its 10 leases for office space in various locations throughout the continental United States to the OCC. In addition, the OCC entered into six new lease occupancy agreements that ranged between two and 193 months, as old leases expired, including a new lease for Headquarters. All of the OCC's leases are treated as operating leases. All annual lease costs under the operating leases are included in the Statements of Net Cost.

Under existing commitments, the minimum yearly lease payments through FY 2017 and thereafter are shown below.

FY 2011 Future Lease Payments (in Thousands)

Year	Amount
2012	$ 45,569
2013	59,915
2014	48,826
2015	45,078
2016	45,657
2017 and beyond	420,088
Total	$ 665,133

FY 2010 Future Lease Payments (in Thousands)

Year	Amount
2011	$ 35,528
2012	24,055
2013	19,654
2014	16,757
2015	13,016
2016 and beyond	43,587
Total	$ 152,597

Note 8—Other Actuarial Liabilities

The OCC's other actuarial liabilities are reported on the Balance Sheets and include the following components.

Federal Employees' Compensation Act

The Federal Employees' Compensation Act provides income and medical cost protection to cover federal civilian employees injured on the job, employees who have incurred a work-related occupational disease, and beneficiaries of employees whose death is attributable to a job-related injury or occupational disease. Claims incurred for benefits for OCC employees covered under the Federal Employees' Compensation Act are administered by the U.S. Department of Labor and later billed to the OCC. FY 2011 and FY 2010 present value of these estimated outflows is calculated using a discount rate of 3.5 percent in the first year and 4.0 percent in subsequent years, and 3.7 percent in the first year and 4.3 percent in subsequent years, respectively.

Pentegra Defined Benefit Plan

According to the provisions of Dodd–Frank, in FY 2011, the OCC assumed the role of benefit administrator for a special retirement system—Pentegra DB Plan. The Pentegra DB Plan

Actuarial Liabilities Category (in Thousands)

Component	FY 2011	FY 2010
Federal Employees' Compensation Act	$ 5,513	$ 1,299
Pentegra DB Plan	9,027	0
Post-retirement life insurance benefits	47,732	24,991
Total actuarial liabilities	**$ 62,272**	**$ 26,290**

is a defined benefit plan that the OTS assumed from its predecessor agency when it was created in 1989. The Pentegra DB Plan is a system in which all costs are paid by the employer into one general account. At retirement, employees may either receive a lump sum or opt for an annuity/lump sum split. There are 299 OTS employees who transferred to the OCC and participate in the Pentegra DB Plan, 542 retirees who receive a Pentegra DB Plan annuity, and 708 separated employees who are deferred vested in the Pentegra DB Plan. Total expenses recognized for the Pentegra DB Plan during FY 2011 were $9.0 million. The unfunded portion of the liability that is actuarially determined was $86.2 million as of September 30, 2011.

Post-retirement Life Insurance Benefits

The OCC sponsors a life insurance benefit plan for current and retired employees. In addition, for one year after the transfer date, the OCC will continue to administer a separate life insurance plan for those OTS employees transferred to the OCC who meet eligibility requirements. The significant increase year over year as shown in the figure above is a result of the transfer of the existing OTS plan liability, which offered higher benefits than the OCC-sponsored plan. Transferred OTS plan participants that remain with the OCC will be converted to the OCC-sponsored plan on July 28, 2012. Liabilities related to the OCC-sponsored plan are significantly lower than the OTS-sponsored plan's. Because the actuarial calculations rely on a variety of factors, it is uncertain whether next year's liability will be reduced once the former OTS employees join the OCC-sponsored plan. The weighted-average discount rate used in determining the accumulated post-retirement benefit obligation was 4.75 percent. Gains or losses owing to changes in actuarial assumptions are amortized over the service life of the plan.

The figure above shows the balance of each of the three components of the OCC's actuarial liabilities.

Net periodic post-retirement benefit costs for life insurance provisions under the plans include the components shown on this page. The total benefit expenses are recognized as program costs in the Statements of Net Cost. Any gains or losses from changes in long-term assumptions used to measure liabilities for post-retirement life insurance benefits are displayed separately on the Statements of Net Cost, as required.

The following table presents a reconciliation of the beginning and ending post-retirement life insurance liability and provides material components of the related expenses.

Reconciliation of Beginning and Ending Post-retirement Liability and the Related Expense (in Thousands)

Change in actuarial and accrued benefits	FY 2011	FY 2010
Actuarial post-retirement liability beginning balance	$ 45,472	$ 21,674
Actuarial expense:		
Normal cost	1,374	747
Interest on the liability balance	2,385	1,198
Actuarial (gain)/loss:		
From experience	495	375
From assumption changes	(691)	1,528
Prior service costs	80	0
Total expense	3,643	3,848
Less amounts paid	(1,383)	(531)
Actuarial post-retirement liability ending balance	$ 47,732	$ 24,991

Note 9—Net Position

Net position represents the net result of operations since inception and includes cumulative amounts related to investments in capitalized assets held by the OCC. The OCC sets aside a portion of its net position as contingency and asset replacement reserves for use at the Comptroller's discretion. In addition, funds are set aside to cover the cost of ongoing operations.

The contingency reserve supports the OCC's ability to accomplish its mission in the case of foreseeable but rare events. Foreseeable but rare events are beyond the control of the OCC and include a major change in the national banking system or the federal savings association industry or, for instance, a fire, flood, or significant impairment of the agency's information technology systems. In addition, reserves are available to address special one-time needs resulting from the regulatory restructuring required by Dodd–Frank, which could include payments for the Pentegra DB Plan. See Note 8.

The asset replacement reserve funds the replacement of information technology investments, leasehold improvements, and furniture replacements for future years. The target level for the replacement reserve is established annually based on the gross value of existing property and equipment plus a growth-rate factor and a margin for market cost adjustments.

The figure below reflects balances for FY 2011 and FY 2010.

Net Position Availability (in Thousands)

Component	FY 2011	FY 2010
Contingency reserve	$ 692,690	$ 425,048
Asset replacement reserve	192,900	192,900
Set aside for ongoing operations:		
Undelivered orders	64,440	58,906
Consumption of assets	112,114	79,408
Capital investments	33,649	29,192
Net position	$ 1,095,793	$ 785,454

Note 10—Net Cost of Operations

The Net Cost of Operations represents the OCC's operating costs deducted from assessments and fees paid by national banks and federal saving associations and from investment interest income earned. The operating costs include the gain or loss from actuarial experience and assumption changes per the guidance in SFFAS No. 33. The imputed financing sources for net cost of operations are reported on the Statements of Changes in Net Position and in Note 12, Reconciliation of Net Cost of Operations to Budget.

The following figure illustrates the OCC's operating expense categories for FY 2011 and FY 2010.

Net Cost of Operations by Expense Category (in Thousands)

	FY 2011	FY 2010
Personnel compensation and benefits	$ 546,739	$ 508,575
Contractual services	115,912	106,476
Rent, communication, and utilities	50,381	49,985
Travel and transportation of persons and things	51,963	48,701
Imputed costs	33,747	32,890
Depreciation	18,437	25,490
Other	20,329	16,354
Total	$ **837,508**	$ **788,471**

Note 11—Imputed Costs and Financing Sources

In accordance with SFFAS No. 5, "Accounting for Liabilities of the Federal Government," federal agencies must recognize the portion of employees' pension and other retirement benefits to be paid by OPM trust funds. These amounts are recorded as imputed costs and imputed financing for other agencies. Annually, OPM provides federal agencies with cost factors for the computation of current year imputed costs. These cost factors are multiplied by the current year salary or number of employees, as applicable, to provide an estimate of the imputed financing that OPM trust funds will provide for each agency.

The imputed costs categories for FY 2011 and FY 2010 are listed in the table below. These imputed costs are included on the Statements of Net Cost. The financing sources absorbed by the OPM are reflected on the Statements of Changes in Net Position and in Note 12, Reconciliation of Net Cost of Operations to Budget.

Imputed Costs Absorbed by the OPM (in Thousands)

Component	FY 2011	FY 2010
Retirement	$ 16,163	$ 18,509
Federal Employees Health Benefits	17,545	14,346
Federal Employees' Group Life Insurance	39	35
Total imputed costs covered by the OPM	$ **33,747**	$ **32,890**

Note 12—Reconciliation of Net Cost of Operations to Budget

The Reconciliation of Net Cost of Operations to Budget demonstrates the relationship between the OCC's proprietary accounting (net cost of operations) and budgetary accounting (net obligations) information. For FY 2011, the statement on the next page shows $25.1 million in excess resources available to finance activities, which is a net increase of $4.0 million over September 30, 2010. This net increase resulted from a $101.4 million increase in resources available (spending authority from offsetting collections) netted against the increase of $84.8 million in resources used (obligations incurred) and the $0.9 million increase in imputed financing, and $11.7 million of OTS resources transferred in. The increase in net resources available is primarily due to increased assessment revenue, while the increase in resources used results from various office space and information technology investments as well as salary and employee benefits, as shown on the next page.

Office of the Comptroller of the Currency
Reconciliation of Net Cost of Operations to Budget
For the Years Ended September 30, 2011 and 2010
(in Thousands)

	FY 2011	FY 2010
Resources used to finance activities		
Budgetary resources obligated		
Obligations incurred	$ 824,994	$ 740,220
Less: spending authority from offsetting collections	(895,505)	(794,109)
Net obligations	(70,511)	(53,889)
Other resources		
Transfer-in without reimbursement (Note 13)	11,675	0
Imputed financing sources (Note 11)	33,747	32,890
Total resources used to finance activities	**(25,089)**	**(20,999)**
Resources used to finance items not part of the net cost of operations		
Change in budgetary resources obligated for goods, services, and benefits ordered but not yet provided	10,903	(792)
Resources that finance the acquisition of assets	(25,821)	(9,359)
Adjustment to net obligated balance that does not affect net cost of operations	(11,675)	0
Total resources used to finance items not part of the net cost of operations	(26,593)	(10,151)
Total resources used to finance the net cost of operations	**$ (51,682)**	**$ (31,150)**
Components of the net cost of operations that will not require or generate resources in the current period		
Components requiring or generating resources in future periods		
Change in deferred revenue	41,071	5,378
Increase in exchange revenue receivable from the public	9,478	1
Total components that will require or generate resources in future periods	50,549	5,379
Components not requiring or generating resources		
Depreciation and amortization	18,437	19,822
Net increase in bond premium	1,742	2,035
Other	(24,741)	5,668
Total components that will not require or generate resources	(4,562)	27,525
Total components of net cost of operations that will not require or generate resources in the current period	**45,987**	**32,904**
Net cost of operations	**$ (5,695)**	**$ 1,754**

Note 13—OTS Transfer

The OTS transfer of assets and liabilities to the OCC was completed on July 21, 2011, in accordance with the guidance outlined in SFFAS No. 7, "Accounting for Revenue and Other Financing Sources and Concepts for Reconciling Budgetary and Financial Accounting." As the receiving entity, the OCC recognized the value of the assets and liabilities transferred-in at the OTS's book value at the time of transfer. Audited amounts transferred in were total assets of $321.0 million, total liabilities of $50.1 million, and total net position of $270.9 million—the majority of which is reflected within the OCC's contingency reserve. The total net position amount represents $259.2 million in budgetary resources, including FBWT amounts transferred in, and $11.7 million in other financing sources, which include property and equipment transferred in.

Note 14—Commitments and Contingencies

The OCC recognizes and discloses contingencies in accordance with SFFAS No. 12, "Recognition of Contingent Liabilities Arising From Litigation." The OCC is party to various administrative proceedings, legal actions, and claims brought against it, including threatened or pending litigation involving federal employment claims, some of which may ultimately result in settlements or decisions against the federal government. As of September 30, 2011, there were four contingencies for litigations involving the OCC. For three of these, there was a reasonable possibility that the OCC could incur a loss of $1.5 million, which comprises $900,000 in back pay plus interest and $600,000 in compensatory damages. For the fourth contingency where the risk of loss was probable, the OCC recorded a liability for FY 2011 of $191,000, which covered an enforcement proceeding plus court costs. As of September 30, 2010, the OCC reported $1.0 million for contingencies where the loss was reasonably possible. There were no contingencies in FY 2010 where the risk of loss was probable. In addition, for FY 2011, the OCC is aware of one potential unasserted claim from a software vendor for approximately $1.1 million. In FY 2010, there were no unasserted claims.

gka,p.c.
Certified Public Accountants
& Consultants

www.gkacpa.com

Independent Auditor's Report on Financial Statements

Inspector General, Department of the Treasury, and
the Comptroller of the Currency:

We have audited the accompanying balance sheets of the Office of the Comptroller of the Currency (OCC) as of September 30, 2011 and 2010, and the related statements of net cost, changes in net position and budgetary resources (hereinafter referred to as "financial statements") for the years then ended. These financial statements are the responsibility of the management of OCC. Our responsibility is to express an opinion on these financial statements based on our audits. We did not audit "transfer-in without reimbursement" of $270.9 million included in the Statement of Changes in Net Position for the year ended September 30, 2011. This represents the net assets of the Office of Thrift Supervision's (OTS), as of July 20, 2011, that were transferred to OCC in accordance with the *Dodd-Frank Wall Street Reform and Consumer Protection Act*. The OTS' financial statements as of and for the period ended July 20, 2011 were audited by another auditor whose report has been furnished to us. Our opinion, insofar as it relates to the amount transferred in from OTS, is based solely on the report of the other auditor.

We conducted our audits in accordance with auditing standards generally accepted in the United States of America; the standards applicable to financial audits contained in *Government Auditing Standards*, issued by the Comptroller General of the United States; and applicable provisions of Office of Management and Budget (OMB) Bulletin No. 07-04, *Audit Requirements for Federal Financial Statements*, as amended. Those standards and OMB Bulletin No. 07-04 require that we plan and perform the audits to obtain reasonable assurance about whether the financial statements are free of material misstatement. An audit includes examining, on a test basis, evidence supporting the amounts and disclosures in the financial statements. An audit also includes assessing the accounting principles used and significant estimates made by management, as well as evaluating the overall financial statement presentation. We believe that our audits and the report of the other auditor provides a reasonable basis for our opinion.

In our opinion, based on our audits and the report of the other auditor, the financial statements referred to above present fairly, in all material respects, the financial position of the OCC as of September 30, 2011 and 2010, and its net costs, changes in net position, and budgetary resources for the years then ended in conformity with accounting principles generally accepted in the United States of America.

1015 18th Street, NW
Suite 200
Washington, DC 20036
Tel: 202-857-1777
Fax: 202-857-1778

Member of the American Institute of Certified Public Accountants

The information in Section Six, pages 43 through 51, and page 76 of OCC's fiscal year 2011 Annual Report is not a required part of the financial statements but is supplementary information required by accounting principles generally accepted in the United States of America. We have applied certain limited procedures, which consisted principally of inquiries of management regarding the methods of measurement and presentation of this information. However, we did not audit this information, and we express no opinion on it.

Our audits were conducted for the purpose of forming an opinion on the financial statements taken as a whole. The information included in Sections One, Two, Three, Four and Five of OCC's fiscal year 2011 Annual Report is presented for purposes of additional analysis and is not a required part of the financial statements. We did not audit this information, and we do not express an opinion on it.

In accordance with *Government Auditing Standards*, we have also issued reports dated October 31, 2011, on our consideration of the OCC's internal control over financial reporting, and on our tests of its compliance with certain provisions of applicable laws, regulations, and contracts. These reports are an integral part of an audit performed in accordance with *Government Auditing Standards*, and should be read in conjunction with this report in considering the results of our audits.

GKA, P.C.

October 31, 2011

www.gkacpa.com

Independent Auditor's Report on Internal Control over Financial Reporting

Inspector General, Department of the Treasury, and
the Comptroller of the Currency:

We have audited the balance sheet and the related statements of net cost, changes in net position, and budgetary resources, hereinafter referred to as "financial statements" of the Office of the Comptroller of the Currency (OCC) as of and for the year ended September 30, 2011, and have issued our report thereon dated October 31, 2011. We did not audit "transfer-in without reimbursement" of $270.9 million included in the Statement of Changes in Net Position for the year ended September 30, 2011. This represents the net assets of the Office of Thrift Supervision's (OTS), as of July 20, 2011, that were transferred to OCC in accordance with the *Dodd-Frank Wall Street Reform and Consumer Protection Act*. The OTS' financial statements as of and for the period ended July 20, 2011 were audited by another auditor whose report has been furnished to us. Our opinion, insofar as it relates to the amount transferred in from OTS, is based solely on the report of the other auditor. We conducted our audit in accordance with auditing standards generally accepted in the United States of America; the standards applicable to financial audits contained in *Government Auditing Standards*, issued by the Comptroller General of the United States; and the applicable provisions of Office of Management and Budget (OMB) Bulletin No. 07-04, *Audit Requirements for Federal Financial Statements*, as amended.

In planning and performing our audit, we considered the OCC's internal control over financial reporting by obtaining an understanding of the design effectiveness of OCC's internal control, determined whether these internal controls had been placed in operation, assessed control risk, and performed tests of controls as a basis for designing our auditing procedures for the purpose of expressing our opinion on the financial statements. We limited our internal control testing to those controls necessary to achieve the objectives described in OMB Bulletin No. 07-04 and *Government Auditing Standards*. We did not test all internal controls relevant to operating objectives as broadly defined by the *Federal Managers' Financial Integrity Act of 1982*, such as those controls relevant to ensuring efficient operations. The objective of our audit was not to provide an opinion on the effectiveness of OCC's internal control over financial reporting. Consequently, we do not provide an opinion on the effectiveness of OCC's internal control over financial reporting.

1015 18th Street, NW
Suite 200
Washington, DC 20036
Tel: 202-857-1777
Fax: 202-857-1778

Member of the American Institute of Certified Public Accountants

Our consideration of the internal control over financial reporting was for the limited purpose described in the preceding paragraph and was not designed to identify all deficiencies in internal control over financial reporting that might be deficiencies, significant deficiencies, or material weaknesses. A deficiency in internal control exists when the design or operation of a control does not allow management or employees, in the normal course of performing their assigned functions, to prevent or detect and correct misstatements on a timely basis. A significant deficiency is a deficiency or combination of deficiencies, in internal control that is less severe than a material weakness, yet important enough to merit attention by those charged with governance.

A material weakness is a deficiency, or a combination of deficiencies, in internal control, such that there is a reasonable possibility that a material misstatement of the entity's financial statements will not be prevented, or detected and corrected on a timely basis.

We did not identify any deficiencies in internal control over financial reporting that we consider to be material weaknesses, as defined above.

We noted certain matters involving internal control and its operation that we reported to Management of OCC in a separate letter dated October 31, 2011.

This report is intended solely for the information and use of the Management of the OCC, the Department of the Treasury Office of Inspector General, the Government Accountability Office, OMB, and the U.S. Congress, and is not intended to be, and should not be used by anyone other than these specified parties. However, this report is a matter of public record and its distribution is not limited.

GKA, P.C.

October 31, 2011

www.gkacpa.com

Independent Auditor's Report on Compliance with Laws and Regulations

The Inspector General, Department of the Treasury, and the Comptroller of the Currency:

We have audited the balance sheets and the related statements of net cost, changes in net position, and budgetary resources, hereinafter referred to as "financial statements" of the Office of the Comptroller of the Currency (OCC) as of and for the years ended September 30, 2011 and 2010, and have issued our report thereon dated October 31, 2011. We did not audit "transfer-in without reimbursement" of $270.9 million included in the Statement of Changes in Net Position for the year ended September 30, 2011. This represents the net assets of the Office of Thrift Supervision's (OTS), as of July 20, 2011, that were transferred to OCC in accordance with the *Dodd-Frank Wall Street Reform and Consumer Protection Act*. The OTS' financial statements as of and for the period ended July 20, 2011 were audited by another auditor whose report has been furnished to us. Our opinion, insofar as it relates to the amount transferred in from OTS, is based solely on the report of the other auditor. We conducted our audits in accordance with auditing standards generally accepted in the United States of America; the standards applicable to financial audits contained in *Government Auditing Standards*, issued by the Comptroller General of the United States; and, the applicable provisions of Office of Management and Budget (OMB) Bulletin No. 07-04, *Audit Requirements for Federal Financial Statements*, as amended.

The management of the OCC is responsible for complying with laws, regulations and contracts applicable to the OCC. As part of obtaining reasonable assurance about whether the OCC's financial statements are free of material misstatement, we performed tests of its compliance with certain provisions of laws, regulations and contracts, noncompliance with which could have a direct and material effect on the determination of financial statement amounts, and certain provisions of other laws and regulations specified in OMB Bulletin No. 07-04, including certain requirements referred to in Section 803(a) of the *Federal Financial Management Improvement Act (FFMIA) of 1996*. We limited our tests of compliance to the provisions described in the preceding sentence, and we did not test compliance with all laws, regulations and contracts applicable to the OCC. However, our objective was not to provide an opinion on overall compliance with laws, regulations and contracts. Accordingly, we do not express such an opinion.

1015 18th Street, NW
Suite 200
Washington, DC 20036
Tel: 202-857-1777
Fax: 202-857-1778

Member of the American Institute of Certified Public Accountants

The results of our tests of compliance with laws, regulations and contracts described in the preceding paragraph, exclusive of FFMIA, disclosed no instances of noncompliance that are required to be reported under *Government Auditing Standards* or OMB Bulletin No. 07-04.

Under FFMIA, we are required to report whether the OCC's financial management systems substantially comply with (1) federal financial management systems requirements, (2) applicable federal accounting standards, and (3) the United States Government Standard General Ledger at the transaction level. To meet this requirement, we performed tests of compliance with FFMIA section 803(a) requirements.

The results of our tests disclosed no instances in which the OCC's financial management systems did not substantially comply with the three requirements discussed in the preceding paragraph.

This report is intended solely for the information and use of the Management of the OCC, the Department of the Treasury Office of Inspector General, the Government Accountability Office, OMB, and U.S. Congress and is not intended to be, and should not be used by anyone other than these specified parties. However, this report is a matter of public record and its distribution is not limited.

GKA, P.C.

October 31, 2011

Performance Measures and Results

The OCC's FY 2011 performance measures, workload indicators, customer service standards, and results are presented in figure 13.

Figure 13: Performance Measures, Workload Indicators, Customer Service Standards, and Results

Strategic goal	Performance measure workload indicator customer service standard	FY 2008	FY 2009	FY 2010	FY 2011 Target	FY 2011 Actual
I. A safe and sound system of national banks and federal savings associations						
	Percentage of national banks and federal savings associations with composite CAMELS rating of 1 or 2[1]	92%	82%	72%	90%	75%
	Rehabilitated problem national banks and federal savings associations as a percentage of the problem national banks one year ago (CAMELS 3, 4, or 5)[1]	47%	29%	22%	40%	22%
	Percentage of national banks and federal savings associations that are well capitalized[1]	99%	86%	91%	95%	93%
	Percentage of critically undercapitalized national banks and federal savings associations on which responsible action is taken within 90 calendar days after they become critically undercapitalized	100%	100%	100%	100%	100%
	Average survey response that the report of examination clearly communicated examination findings, significant issues, and the corrective actions management needed to take[2]	1.28	1.34	1.47	≤ 1.75	1.45
II. Fair access to financial services and fair treatment of national bank and federal savings association customers						
	Percentage of national banks and federal savings associations with consumer compliance rating of 1 or 2. For institutions with assets over $10 billion, these ratings will reflect only those laws and regulations for which the OCC has enforcement and supervisory authority.	97%	97%	96%	94%	94%
	Percentage of community banks that are within one year of their first Intermediate Small Bank or Large Bank Community Reinvestment Act examination for which the OCC offers to provide consultation on community development opportunities	100%	100%	100%	100%	100%
	Percentage of consumer complaints closed within 60 calendar days of receipt	12%	8%	3%	80%	30%
	Number of consumer complaints opened/closed during the fiscal year	41,656/ 30,986	58,810/ 32,533	80,336/ 79,660	72,000/ 70,000	84,557/ 84,773
III. A flexible legal and regulatory framework that enables national banks and federal savings associations to provide a full, competitive array of financial services consistent with statutory and prudential safety and soundness constraints						
	Percentage of external legal opinions issued within established time frames	92%	88%	85%	86%	91%
	Number of external legal opinions issued during the fiscal year	73	53	64	60	77
	Percentage of licensing applications and notices filed electronically	46%	51%	44%	40%	53%
	Number of licensing applications and notices filed electronically during the fiscal year	1,525	1,681	1,440	1,200	1,610
	Percentage of licensing applications and notices completed within established time frames	95%	95%	96%	95%	97%
	Number of licensing applications and notices completed during the fiscal year[3]	1,843	1,471	1,344	1,200	1,382
	Average survey rating of the overall licensing services provided by the OCC[4]	1.22	1.25	1.15	≤ 1.5	1.31
IV. A competent, highly motivated, and diverse workforce that makes effective use of OCC resources						
	Total OCC costs relative to every $100,000 in assets regulated	$8.39	$8.81	$9.28	$9.22	$8.49

Source: OCC data for all fiscal years.

[1] These performance measures for fiscal year 2011 are below target primarily because of the difficult economic situation the entire financial industry is facing. The OCC continues to closely monitor the capital levels and performance of all its banks and, when necessary, initiates formal and informal agreements to enhance its level of supervision.

[2] The examination survey is based on a five-point scale, in which 1 indicates complete agreement and 5 indicates complete disagreement.

[3] The number of total licensing filings has declined from the previous fiscal year because the number is based on actual applications received, which also declined.

[4] The licensing survey is based on a five-point scale, in which 1 indicates outstanding and 5 indicates significantly deficient.

Improper Payments Elimination and Recovery Act

The Improper Payments Elimination and Recovery Act of 2010, as implemented by the OMB, requires federal agencies to review all programs and activities annually and identify those that may be susceptible to significant erroneous payments. The OCC analyzed payments (excluding payroll) made during FY 2011 and identified 52 erroneous payments requiring adjustments totaling $17,060. Erroneous payments are identified and monitored daily to ensure prompt recovery. The underlying causes and contributing factors are identified quickly, and control measures are implemented to prevent additional erroneous payments.

The OCC corrected and recovered all erroneous payments made during the year. Figure 14 summarizes the OCC's erroneous payments for FY 2011 and FY 2010.

Figure 14: Erroneous Payments

	FY 2011	FY 2010
Number of payments	52	26
Dollar value of adjustments	$17,060	$29,163

Source: OCC data.

Assurance Statement

The Office of the Comptroller of the Currency (OCC) made a conscientious effort during fiscal year (FY) 2011 to meet the internal control requirements of the Federal Managers' Financial Integrity Act (FMFIA), the Federal Financial Management Improvement Act (FFMIA), and Office of Management and Budget (OMB) Circular A-123.

The OCC's systems of management control are designed to ensure that

a) programs achieve their intended results;

b) resources are used in accordance with the agency's mission;

c) programs and resources are protected from waste, fraud, and mismanagement;

d) laws and regulations are followed;

e) controls are sufficient to minimize improper or erroneous payments;

f) performance information is reliable;

g) system security is in substantial compliance with relevant requirements;

h) continuity of operations planning in critical areas is sufficient to reduce risk to reasonable levels; and

i) financial management systems are in compliance with federal financial systems standards, i.e., FMFIA Section 4 and the FFMIA.

I am providing unqualified assurance that the above listed management control objectives were achieved by the OCC without material weakness during FY 2011. Specifically, this assurance is provided relative to Sections 2 and 4 of the FMFIA.

I am also reporting substantial compliance with the requirements imposed by the FFMIA.

The OCC conducted its assessment of the effectiveness of internal control over financial reporting, which includes the safeguarding of assets and compliance with applicable laws and regulations, in accordance with the requirements of Appendix A of OMB Circular A-123. Based on the results of this evaluation, the OCC can provide unqualified assurance that its internal control over financial reporting was operating effectively as of June 30, 2011, and no material weaknesses were found in the design or operation of the internal control over financial reporting.

I also provide unqualified assurance that our supervision programs achieved intended results despite the extraordinary challenges that continued to confront the national banking system.

The nation has weathered the worst financial crisis since the Great Depression, but it may be years before all of its ill effects are behind us. The Dodd–Frank Wall Street Reform and Consumer Protection Act took important steps to strengthen the financial system and guard against future crises, and the OCC is implementing its responsibilities regarding those safeguards as quickly and effectively as possible.

The OCC is involved in 96 individual projects stemming from Dodd–Frank, including interagency rulemakings that will significantly impact our financial system.

Our biggest single task this fiscal year has been to integrate the staff and functions of the Office of Thrift Supervision (OTS) into the OCC.[46] The OCC welcomed 670 OTS employees into policy and field units in offices around the country, successfully moving to a single regulator for national banks and federal savings associations. We need former OTS staff's talent and experience to help fulfill our combined supervisory mission.

To share OCC supervisory expectations with federal savings associations, we corresponded with thrift industry executives through a series of information letters. We hosted 17 meetings for more than 1,000 thrift executives, who were pleased that the OCC will maintain the OTS exam cycle and use its historical supervisory information to reduce regulatory burden.

Pursuant to Dodd–Frank, the OCC established the Office of Minority and Women Inclusion (OMWI) to provide executive direction, set policies, and oversee OCC efforts encouraging diversity in management, employment, and business activities. OMWI workforce initiatives will play a significant role in continuing to keep the OCC atop the list of "Best Places to Work."

We are engaged in several rulemakings affecting federal savings associations, including

---

[46] On July 21, 2011, the OTS independently submitted its final FY 2011 Assurance Statement to the Secretary of the Treasury for the period of October 1, 2010, through July 20, 2011.

republishing as OCC rules those OTS regulations that the OCC has authority to administer and enforce going forward. We continue to review those regulations, as well as our own, for added improvements. We have published a final rule addressing areas important for continuity of supervision, including assessments of federal savings associations and completed rulemaking to revise rules on preemption and visitorial powers. Dodd–Frank calls for a number of other rulemakings, and we have proposed interagency rules to address credit-risk retention, incentive compensation, proprietary trading, and margin and capital requirements for covered swap entities.

In FY 2011, considerable effort was also devoted to the transfer of supervisory responsibilities to the new Consumer Financial Protection Bureau (CFPB) and to our participation in the work of the Financial Stability Oversight Council, which will be an important venue for averting and addressing future market disruptions.

The OCC provided considerable support for the CFPB standup and worked with the new agency to harmonize our complementary supervisory roles. As part of its support, the OCC assisted the CFPB in developing its procurement and personnel management processes.

To assist the CFPB's supervision requirements, we executed a memorandum of understanding to allow sharing of reports of examination, supervisory letters, information on enforcement actions, and other important confidential information. We also established an OCC steering committee to facilitate coordination and communication with the CFPB on consumer protection issues affecting national banks and federal savings associations. The OCC continues to provide transitional support for other CFPB functions, including consumer complaints. In fact, the OCC's Customer Assistance Group has been handling consumer complaints about the large banks now under CFPB supervision while the CFPB builds its own capacity.

Analytical Basis of Assurance Statement

The OCC evaluated its management controls in accordance with the FY 2011 Secretary's Assurance Statement Guidance of July 1, 2011, and considered the following guidance:

- OMB Circular A-127, Financial Management Systems;
- OMB Circular A-130 Revised, Management of Federal Information Resources; and
- Treasury Directive 40-04, Treasury Internal (Management) Control Program.

Information considered in our control assessment included the following:

- FMFIA certifications submitted by each Executive Committee member;
- FFMIA certification submitted by our Chief Financial Officer;

- The OCC's Strategic Risk Management Plan;
- Results of internal control testing under OMB Circular A-123, Appendix A;
- Executive Committee descriptions of business unit quality management programs;
- Results of control self-assessments completed by OCC managers in FY 2011;
- Audit reports and evaluations issued by the Government Accountability Office (GAO) and the Office of the Inspector General;
- Results of other external and internal reviews;
- Improper Payments Information Act risk assessment submitted to the U.S. Department of the Treasury in June 2011;
- GAO Core Financial System Requirements Checklist;
- FFMIA Risk Model and Financial Management System Self-Assessment Checklists submitted to the Treasury Department in July 2011;
- Unqualified and timely audit opinion on FY 2010 financial statements; and
- Certified public accountant Gardiner, Kamya and Associates' status report of October 14, 2011, on the FY 2011 financial statement audit.

John Walsh

John Walsh
Acting Comptroller
of the Currency
November 3, 2011

Abbreviations

ATM	automated teller machines
CAMELS	capital, asset quality, management, earnings, liquidity, and sensitivity to market risk
CARE	Coalition of African-American Regulatory Employees
CMP	civil money penalty
CSRS	Civil Service Retirement System
CFPB	Consumer Financial Protection Bureau
FASAB	Federal Accounting Standards Advisory Board
FBWT	fund balance with Treasury
FDIC	Federal Deposit Insurance Corporation
FEGLI	Federal Employees' Group Life Insurance
FEHB	Federal Employees Health Benefits
FERS	Federal Employees Retirement System
FFMIA	Federal Financial Management Improvement Act
FMFIA	Federal Managers' Financial Integrity Act
FSOC	Financial Stability Oversight Council
FY	fiscal year
GAAP	generally accepted accounting principles
GAO	Government Accountability Office
GLSA	Gay, Lesbian, and Straight Alliance
HOLA	Hispanic Organization for Leadership and Advancement
ITS	Information Technology Services
LSS	Lean Six Sigma
NAPA	Network of Asian Pacific Americans
OCC	Office of the Comptroller of the Currency
OM	Office of Management
OMB	Office of Management and Budget
OMWI	Office of Minority and Women Inclusion
OPM	Office of Personnel Management

OTS	Office of Thrift Supervision
QRM	qualified residential mortgages
SFFAS	Statement of Federal Financial Accounting Standards
SFAS	Statement of Financial Accounting Standard
USC	U.S. Code

Index

preemption standard, 3, 12–13, 79

sources of revenue, inside front cover, 46, 49, 56–57

workforce, inside front cover, 23–24, 35, 56, 76, 78

Office of Thrift Supervision (OTS)

communications and outreach, 2–3, 27

Dodd–Frank. *See* Dodd–Frank Wall Street Reform and Consumer Protection Act of 2010

employees, inside front cover

federal savings associations, inside front cover, i–ii, 5, 7–8, 9, 12–13, 14, 15–16, 20, 24, 25, 26, 29, 30, 33, 34, 38, 40, 43–44, 46, 47, 49, 50, 51, 56, 58, 61, 65, 76, 78–79

former headquarters, 63

integration into OCC, 2, 4, 11–12, 24, 25, 27

Joint Implementation Plan, 11

pilot examinations, 12

policy integration project, 11, 25–26

preemption standard, 3, 12

staffing plan, 12

transfer, assets and liabilities, 44, 45, 46, 47

transfer date, 2, 3, 7, 11, 13, 43, 45, 47, 50, 56, 59, 62, 63, 64, 69, 78

Ombudsman, 20, 35

OTS–OCC integration. *See* OCC–OTS integration

Otto, Bert, 27

P

performance measures and results, 9, 29, 76

policy integration project, 11, 25–26

preemption

Barnett preemption standard, 3

Cuomo v. *the Clearing House Association*, 13

state visitorial and enforcement power, 12, 13, 79

prepaid access, 21

Privacy Act, 24

prompt corrective action, 41

proprietary trading. *See* Dodd–Frank Wall Street Reform and Consumer Protection Act of 2010

Public Affairs Department, OCC, 33, 35

public service announcements, 19, 20

Q

qualified residential mortgages (QRM). *See* mortgages

R

real estate, 5, 7, 10, 29

appraisals and evaluation guidelines, 10

commercial, 7, 16, 29

residential, 7, 10, 18, 29

reconciliation of net cost of operations to budget, 66, 67–68

records integration and Freedom of Information Act, 24

Comptroller of the Currency
Administrator of National Banks

US Department of the Treasury

www.ingramcontent.com/pod-product-compliance
Lightning Source LLC
Chambersburg PA
CBHW080317290526
45790CB00005B/2070